Teaching Mathematics Vocabulary in Context

Windows, Doors, and Secret Passageways

Miki Murray

HEINEMANN
Portsmouth, NH

Heinemann

361 Hanover Street

Portsmouth, NH 03801–3912

www.heinemann.com

Offices and agents throughout the world

The author and publisher wish to thank those who have generously given permission to reprint borrowed material:

The triangle problem in the Introduction is reprinted by permission from the *2001–2002 MATHCOUNTS School Handbook* edited by Kristen L. Chandler. Published by MATHCOUNTS Foundation.

The natural-numbers problem in Chapter 2 is reprinted by permission from the *2002–2003 MATHCOUNTS School Handbook* edited by Kristen L. Chandler. Published by MATHCOUNTS Foundation.

Credit lines continue on page 196.

Library of Congress Cataloging-in-Publication Data

Murray, Miki.

    Teaching mathematics vocabulary in context : windows, doors, and secret passageways / Miki Murray.

      p. cm.

    Includes bibliographical references and index.

    ISBN 0-325-00634-2 (alk. paper)

    1. Mathematics—Study and teaching (Middle school). 2. Mathematics—Terminology. I. Title.

    QA11.2.M87 2004

    510′.71′2—dc22

                                                    2003018827

Editor: Victoria Merecki

Production coordinator: Elizabeth Valway

Production service: Denise A. Botelho

Cover design: Lisa Fowler

Cover image: Carol & Mike Werner/Superstock

Composition: House of Equations, Inc.

Manufacturing: Steve Bernier

Printed in the United States of America on acid-free paper

13 12 11 10 09 VP 6 7 8 9 10

This book is dedicated to my dear friend and former colleague Shirley Dabora, and the hundreds of math students from Michigan, Connecticut, and Maine who taught me about learning mathematics.

Contents

FOREWORD BY MARI MURI   vii

ACKNOWLEDGMENTS   x

INTRODUCTION—WHY STUDY VOCABULARY IN MATH CLASS?   1

Section One—Establishing the Role of Mathematics Vocabulary

1 Setting the Stage   11
2 Speaking Mathematics   35
3 What About Deliberate Vocabulary Work?   60

Section Two—Pushing the Vocabulary: Going for Breadth and Depth Through Writing

4 Problem-Solving Write-Ups   85
5 Mathematical Reflections   102
6 Expanding Vocabulary with Journals and Homework   116
7 Self-Assessment as a Vocabulary Development Tool   131
8 Mathematics Vocabulary: A Focus for Writing   142

Section Three—The Vocabulary Aftermath

9   Creating Mathematics Poetry   153

10   Putting Vocabulary Learning Strategies Into Context   168

EPILOGUE   175

BIBLIOGRAPHY   187

INDEX   193

foreword

E ven though it had been years since I reviewed manuscripts for the
National Council of Teachers of Mathematics (NCTM) publication,
Mathematics Teaching in the Middle School, when Miki Murray asked me
if I would a review a manuscript that she had prepared for possible submission to a refereed math journal, I couldn't say no. As a member of the edi-
torial panel of NCTM, my personal mission was to encourage and work with
classroom teachers, grades 5 through 8, to get their articles published. Miki
was a perfect candidate.

The focus on grades K through 8 education in this country has been
primarily on the language arts—especially reading and more recently, writing. Getting students to read and understand what they read is critical. These
skills are necessary in order for students to do well in school and to become
productive citizens. But much of this attention on reading and writing has
been at the expense of another subject that is equally necessary for people
to function in our society—mathematics.

Miki's idea for the article centered on students becoming more familiar with the vocabulary of mathematics. By doing so, they would be better
able to comprehend problems and carry on discourse about their understanding of problems—the first, and necessary, step to problem solving.
Being able to communicate orally and in writing with appropriate language
solidifies the learner's understanding of the significant aspects of the
problem.

Her manuscript was rich with ideas for developing the vocabulary of mathematics, for using student work to demonstrate how vocabulary is acquired, and for making student understanding come alive. In fact, it was too comprehensive for a short journal article. I offered some suggestions for getting her work down to a few pages, but also encouraged her to work with a publisher to expand all of her wonderful ideas in a book.

Indeed, what you will see in this book are a highly talented teacher's ways of integrating mathematics with language arts and how that leads to improved student understanding of both subjects.

Lest you think that acquisition of vocabulary is trivial, think of the word *supplementary*. In daily usage, *supplementary* refers to "something added, especially to make up for a lack." In mathematics (geometry) this same term is used to describe two angles the sum of whose measures is 180 degrees. The same word has different meanings in everyday language and in mathematics; the meaning in mathematics is very specific. Different meanings of words are common in everyday language and mathematics, for example *similar, slope, transformation, odd,* and many others.

Miki expects her students to write regularly about the mathematics they are learning. Her students learn (and you will, too) how to organize their work, especially the vocabulary and writing, in a binder. Also included are powerful reflections by students on their own learning. These reflections help students develop their vocabulary. Maintaining this mathematics binder becomes second nature!

As you follow Miki's students in their journey to develop mathematics vocabulary, you will find that theory and practice are brought to life in student work samples. Also, much of the theory and practice included are supported by research. In fact, research seems to underlie all of Miki's teaching. She has done a masterful job in bringing all this information together in one place.

In this book, you will fall in love with Anne, a gifted middle-school student who will astonish you with her insights into the richness of mathematics vocabulary and her willingness to share her work. Anne is one of the inspirations that led Miki to write this book.

Anne, and students from Miki's classes over several years, contributed to the richness of this book. You will see student examples liberally sprinkled throughout this text. They support and bring to life the author's belief in the importance of her teaching and her high expectations for student learning. Not all students were initially eager and ready to embrace the learning of vocabulary and writing in mathematics—after all, math is supposed to be about numbers. But as the school year progressed, even the most reluctant students produced products that showed evidence of how attention to vocabulary of mathematics enhanced their learning and understanding of mathematics.

Each chapter begins with quotes from well-known authors, including mathematicians. These quotes set the stage for the description of Miki's instructional strategies. In the NCTM *Professional Teaching Standards for School Mathematics* (1991), discourse is an important component for promoting student understanding and teacher understanding of what students are saying. The importance of discourse is clearly evident on page after page of Miki's description of her teaching. Students' understanding of mathematics is illustrated through their oral and written work, which, in turn, allows the teacher to assess student understanding. This ongoing monitoring helps teachers make instructional decisions for future lessons.

Miki describes how the development of each student's vocabulary helps to promote discussions in the classroom—among teacher and students, and among students. She describes her own style of questioning; she also cites readily available, additional resources to help improve questioning techniques.

I'm thrilled that Miki took the time to prepare this extended manuscript. I learned so much about teaching and learning from reading about what goes on in her classroom. I am in awe of the work produced by her students—even the most reluctant ones. I am confident you will have the same reactions!

Mari Muri, Mathematics Consultant
Connecticut State Department of Education (retired)
NCTM Board of Directors (2003–2006)

Acknowledgments

I teach from one day to the next based on the needs that emerge from my students as we work within a framework of curriculum goals. In this manner students have been at the heart of my learning about teaching math. It is appropriate then that a student, Anne Atwell-McLeod, who spent her seventh and eighth grade math time in my class, is at the core of my work here. She tipped the first domino that cascaded into this book.

I wish to thank Glenda Lappan for suggesting I share Anne's poetry about mathematics through a journal article. I am grateful to Mari Muri who reviewed my initial work and graciously asked me to say more about the vocabulary practices that encouraged the kind of mathematical understanding and power evidenced in the work of my students. My deep gratitude goes to Mari for the encouragement that propelled me forward and for the culminating act of generous collaboration represented by her foreword.

My growth as a math teacher has been nourished by several generations of students, hundreds of colleagues, gracious caring parents, and excellent professional development opportunities. I am deeply grateful to all of the teachers, parents, and students—particularly those students who allowed their work to clarify and illustrate the ideas presented throughout the book.

Three professional development programs have been vital to my evolution. The first is MATHTEQ, a grant developed by Kay Gilliland and the amazing staff of EQUALS and FAMILY MATH at the Lawrence Hall of Science in Berkeley, CA. They welcomed me with open arms in 1988 and taught me volumes about equity in general and in the mathematics classroom in particular. They initiated a supportive and responsive lifetime dialogue about professional concerns. The second is Marilyn Burns, whose phone conversations, letters, Math Solutions workshops, publications, conference presentations, and videos have been a guide and an inspiration for the past fifteen years. She and her associates are passionate, caring professionals who exemplify 'respect for classroom teachers.' My remaining critical professional development connection is the series of programs initiated by the Mathematics and Mathematics Education Departments at Michigan State University. Glenda Lappan and her late colleague, Bill Fitzgerald, led me and several teammates from Bath, Maine, into the National Science Foundation-supported Middle Grades Mathematics Project professional development program in 1988. This amazing opportunity to work with teachers and mathematics educators from around the nation and the world helped me see mathematics with new eyes and new understanding, and continues today through the development and implementation of *Connected Mathematics*. I am forever indebted to these remarkable professional colleagues for sharing their amazing insights and knowledge, and for their generous support.

I am enormously grateful to Nancie Atwell who invited me to return to the classroom as the seventh- and eighth-grade mathematics teacher at the Center for Teaching and Learning (CTL) in 1997. CTL is the private K–8 demonstration school Nancie created in Edgecomb, ME. After ten years of work in professional development, CTL provided a perfect environment for me to implement my ideas to the fullest and adapt them to a multigrade classroom. My helping teacher, Katie Rittershaus, provided invaluable classroom support, probing questions, and the constant prodding that incubated the idea of writing about my teaching. And Nancie was right there urging me to write a book to document the work I was doing in the classroom. Without her fine insights and generous encouragement I would not have done this work.

I am deeply appreciative of my husband Donald for his constant support, many patient hours keeping the technology working, and forever telling me I could do it. I must also acknowledge the important role played by my snuggly standard poodle Starr, who came into my life as the project was generated. She and my friend and neighbor Phyllis walked and talked me through the struggles of a beginning writer—I am, after all, a math teacher.

I am indebted to Toby Gordon who gave me a concrete organizational scheme for initiating this project. I also wish to thank Alan Huisman for smoothing the edges with his extraordinary editing as the final revisions emerged.

I am beholden to Leigh Peake who had enough faith in the possibilities of my thesis to introduce me to my collegial editor Victoria Merecki. I cannot imagine having written this book without her. Victoria was with me every step of the way with guidance, encouragement, and suggestions as I ventured through unknown territory. She is the kind and gentle collaborator who brought the project to fruition. Victoria has my ultimate gratitude.

Introduction: Why Study Vocabulary in Math Class?

Any fool can know. The point is to understand.
                                    —ALBERT EINSTEIN

*I'm a word person. Numbers don't mean anything to
me unless there are words behind them—reasons I
can verbalize.*

                    —ANNE, eighth grader

For students like Anne, words are the window to the world. Anne's observation underscores the potentially powerful connection between developing a strong mathematics vocabulary and developing meaningful mathematical knowledge. In fact, it's the thesis of this book—how vocabulary acquisition impacts the learning of mathematics.

Middle schoolers—students whose ability to reason abstractly is growing dramatically—in particular need to communicate mathematically in an increasingly sophisticated way. Deliberate and careful attention to acquiring and using the vocabulary of mathematics, with its wondrously specific technical language, is a must. This is a dramatic change, and one in which teachers play a crucial role.

The focus on vocabulary in my mathematics instruction has been triggered by subtle clues provided by my students. Jacob, for example, is always somewhat disdainful of my daily math vocabulary warm-ups. Working on a math challenge one afternoon, he put forth a great deal of effort, confident that a solution was at hand. Eventually frustrated, he practically demanded that others explain how *they* were solving the problem. He was amazed to learn that he had, in his own words, "wasted" an incredible amount of effort because he didn't know the meaning of two "simple little words" in the following problem:

> Triangle ABC and triangle DEF are similar right triangles. The *two legs* of triangle ABC are 5 cm and 6 cm in length. If the area of triangle DEF is 135 sq cm, what is the number of centimeters in the length of the *longer leg* of triangle DEF? (*2001–2002 MATHCOUNTS School Handbook,* 42 author's italics)

Jacob was unaware that "two legs" meant anything special related to a right triangle, so he simply ignored the words as not important to the problem. He did, however, know that the hypotenuse is the *longest* side of a right triangle and was working hard to determine the length of the hypotenuse for triangle DEF. Not knowing the vocabulary made the problem impossible for Jacob to correctly interpret or solve.

But long before Jacob, I became convinced that purposefully studying vocabulary is a key element of mathematics. During my early years as a classroom teacher, I experienced days of dismay in my first fourth-grade math class. The children were "borrowing" and "carrying" in meaningless mechanical computations with no apparent understanding of why. They did not demonstrate any knowledge of place value or the number system. I asked myself, what will tune these kids in to the truly important parts of the math work? How can I get them to focus on the big ideas, such as place value, and use details, such as renaming, to support their computation work? Do they really comprehend what they're doing with paper and pencil? Can they explain the meaning of every mark they make and why it contributes to a solution? How can they develop the necessary skills in mindful rather than mindless ways? Are the lessons necessary or helpful? Why and how? Are students simply parroting what I do and say?

With these questions as my guide, I struggled to develop classroom rituals that would engage students with the content. I also needed ways to know that the engagement was genuine. Important clues came from the few confident students. Their self-assurance was obvious. What could I learn from them that I could use to help others? I realized that they understood and used the specialized vocabulary associated with the math they were doing, where every word—even the little ones like *of, by, in, on, and, or*—clarifies a given situation, where *similar* means more than having an analogous relationship. These students enjoyed using correct terminology when talking about even the most mundane computation. When they had opportunities to explain their thinking about why answers made sense, they exhibited a sense of control and power. These students were "mathematically powerful."

While working to implement the National Council of Teachers of Mathematics' *Curriculum and Evaluation Standards for School Mathematics* (1989), Ruth Parker of the Mathematics Education Collaborative described mathematically powerful students this way:

♦ Understand the power of mathematics as a tool for making sense of situations, information, and events in their world.

♦ Are persistent in their search for solutions to complex, messy, or ill-defined tasks.

♦ Enjoy doing mathematics and find the pursuit of solutions to complex problems both challenging and engaging.

♦ Understand mathematics is not just arithmetic.

♦ Make connections within and among mathematical ideas and domains.

♦ Have a disposition to search for patterns and relationships.

♦ Make conjectures and investigate them.

♦ Have "number sense" and are able to make sense of numerical information.

♦ Use algorithmic thinking, and are able to estimate and mentally compute.

♦ Work both independently and collaboratively as problem posers and problem solvers.

- Communicate and justify their thinking and ideas both orally and in writing.
- Use available tools to solve problems and to examine mathematical ideas.

How can we create classrooms that make mathematical power a reality for all students? Clearly, all students—not just a few—need to be mathematically literate. Just as clearly, it will take something other than the traditional nineteenth- and twentieth-century approaches to teaching mathematics to prepare students for the current technical world, let alone the unknown challenges that are surely in their future. It is my conviction that an important way to ensure the development of mathematically powerful students is to build a strong foundation in mathematics vocabulary.

I am supported by a record of research reaching as far back as 1944 that indicates a clear connection between vocabulary development and success in mathematics:

- In *Mathematics Spoken Here*, Lelon Capps and Martha Gage (1987) summarize research on the role of language and vocabulary in the learning of mathematics. They conclude that "mathematics vocabulary, studied in context, has a profound effect on performance" (5). In particular they cite a 1944 study by Harry C. Johnson of the effect of learning vocabulary on solving problems. The study, reported in the *Journal of Educational Research*, found that "learning vocabulary allowed the experimental group to outperform the control group to a significant degree" (Capps, 4–5). They also cite W. J. Lyda and T. M. Duncan's claim in a 1967 *Arithmetic Teacher*, that "direct study of quantitative vocabulary contributes significantly to better mathematical word problem-solving ability" (Capps, 5).

- Janet Allen (1999) advocates direct vocabulary instruction in all content areas because it supports learning new concepts, deeper conceptual understanding, and more effective communication. She cites evidence from a synthesis of research on vocabulary acquisition done by Baker, Simons, and Kameenui (1995). The report documents a reciprocal relationship between conceptual understanding and vocabulary knowledge in any content area (Allen, 29).

◆ Camille Blachowicz and Peter Fisher (1996) preface their textbook *Teaching Vocabulary in All Classrooms* by saying that research as well as practice confirms how important learning vocabulary is, in all content areas, in achieving the broader goal of acquiring content knowledge.

In fact, tracing the use of terminology by students is one of the ways we have of assessing conceptual development. How else do we assess a student's comfort with a concept except as she or he explains the solution to a problem in which the concept is embedded? The accurate use of the vocabulary is an effective measure of conceptual understanding.

Let's look at two examples. Tyler's writing (Figure I–1) is convincing evidence that he understands prisms, surface area, and the maximum and minimum surface areas possible when volume is held constant. Tyler is comfortable with both the vocabulary and the concepts, and it is not possible to draw a line between the two. On the other hand, Forrest's writing (Figure I–2) is not convincing evidence of his understanding. He has used related vocabulary for working with variables, but he has not connected them to problem solutions or examples. Forrest uses "slope" informally and is only beginning to understand the concepts involved in the investigation and their relationships to each other.

The chapters that follow describe techniques, venues, and challenges I've used to support vocabulary acquisition. They include all aspects of a fully implemented mathematics curriculum: establishing the environment, class work (including individual, small-group, and whole-group work), homework, assessments, real-world connections, problem solving and explanations, creative writing, and parent conferences. These strategies have evolved from my personal teaching and learning, which is grounded in reflection: What works? What doesn't work? Why?

The collection of strategies represents the culmination of a long teaching career. Teachers just beginning to consider a more serious role for mathematics vocabulary in their classrooms are invited to pick and choose

Mathematical Reflection 2, 3

In these two investegutions, we worked with rectangular and non-rectangular prisms. First, we arranged cubes into the shapes of rectangular prisms. While doing this, we found that we could reduce the surface area of a prism but still have the same amount of volume. We found that the more cube-like the prism was, the less surface area there was. This is because the cubes are not showing many faces. If you had (one cube high and wid) a long, skinny, and short prism, you would have a lot of surface area because every cube would show at least four sides. Here is an example. If you have 2 prisms, both with a volume of 8, you could have two different surface area. You could have a cube—2x2x2, or a long, skinny, and short prism— 1x1x8. To find the surface area of them, it will help to draw them. Here they are.

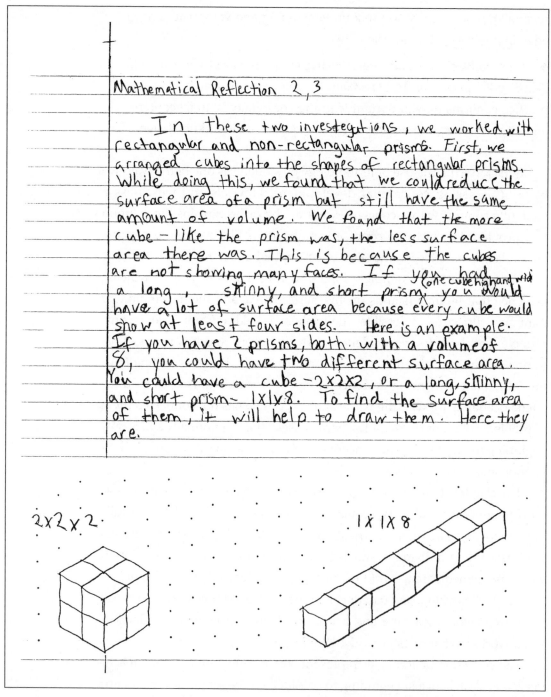

2x2x2   1x1x8

FIGURE I–1   *Tyler's Mathematical Reflection on the Surface Area and Volume of Prisms*

I will start with the 2x2x2 prism. I know that all of sides are the same, so all that I have to do is figure out one side and multiply it by 6. To find the surface area of one face, I will multiply its two dimensions together to get $4u^2$, which I then multiply by 6 to get to $24u^2$. That is the surface area of the 2x2x2 prism.

The 1x1x8 prism is not as easy. There are two different size faces.² 1x1's, and and 4 1x8's. The 1x1 faces are easy because 1x1=1 x2 (because there are two)= 2^u. The four 1x8 are harder 1x8 = 8 x4 (because there are four 1x8 faces) = $32u^2$ $32+2$ a total surface area of $34u^2$ Its surface area is $10u^2$ larger than the 2x2x2 prism, but has the same volume.

Next, we developed strategies for finding the volume of both rectangular and non-rectangular prisms. While we were making these strategies, we found that the number of unit cubes that are needed to fill a prism, and the volume are the same.

We also made a strategy to find the volume of any prism. First, you have to find the surface area of the bottom. Next, you have to find the height. Then you multiply them together to get the volume. The surface area of the bottom will tell you how many cubes will fit on the bottom, then the height will tell you how many cubes will fit.

FIGURE I–1   *continued.*

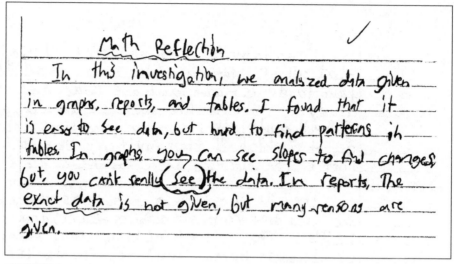

FIGURE I–2   *Forrest's Mathematical Reflection Comparing Tables, Graphs, and Narrative Reports*

elements to try. Select as few or as many as seem appropriate to your current teaching situation. Then reflect upon the results.

When practical and applicable, the text is accompanied by examples of student work produced within a curriculum that values a growing proficiency with the language of mathematics. These students recognize math everywhere—they know it, they talk about it, they write about it, and they use it in powerful ways because learning the vocabulary allows them to grow steadily in their ability to communicate mathematically.

Establishing the Role of Mathematics Vocabulary

*I noticed that most students are not good at using
mathematical terminology. Many of them haven't
realized that technical terms aren't just arbitrary
syllables designed to make their lives more difficult. . . .
Historically speaking, there used to be less of a
separation between mathematics and language than
there is now.*

—STEVEN SCHWARTZMAN (1994, 1)

CHAPTER 1

Setting the Stage

Too often, the rationale for what we do in the classroom isn't obvious to students, and students don't have access to the information. We as teachers must clarify the reasons for our instructional choices and find ways to make them clear to students so they are informed and motivated.

—MARILYN BURNS (1995, 130)

Mathematical communication requires more than mastery of numbers and symbols. It requires the development of a common language using vocabulary that is understood by all. Brain research tells us that we can expect the seeds of math and logic—basic counting, for example—to be planted before age one (Jensen 1998). It is also known that better language skills are developed when parents talk to infants frequently using adult words. It would be ideal if mathematics vocabulary was routinely connected to the spatial and number relationships that feed a child's developing brain network.

Unfortunately technical math terms aren't part of everyday social interaction. The United Kingdom's Mathematical Association (1987) comments that "mathematical language may play little part in the conversation of the home. . . . Many children are disadvantaged linguistically in mathematics in comparison with other areas of their experience. Most children, therefore, need particular help with language in mathematics" (6). The association concurs that mathematical thinking rests on basic relationships and the associated vocabulary.

Zal Usiskin (1996), a leading American mathematician and mathematics educator, characterizes mathematics itself as a language. He sees the study of the teaching and learning of language as providing useful guidance for teaching and learning mathematics. He feels that if mathematics were treated as a native language rather than a foreign language, using repeated exposure and immersion *"everyone* could learn a significant amount of mathematics" (241). Children learn their native language from those around them. However, mathematics vocabulary doesn't find its way easily into the developing child's social environment.

Clearly, the classroom will have to compensate for the neglected language factor, and the National Council of Teachers of Mathematics (NCTM) has long recognized that fact. Included in NCTM's landmark *Curriculum and Evaluation Standards for School Mathematics* (1989) is the following statement:

> Middle school students should have many opportunities to use language to communicate their mathematical ideas. . . . Writing and talking about their thinking clarifies students' ideas and gives the teacher valuable information from which to make instructional decisions. Emphasizing communication in a mathematics class helps shift the classroom from an environment in which students are totally dependent on the teacher to one in which students assume more responsibility for validating their own thinking. (78–79)

Such high standards for mathematical communication imply the need for students to develop an increasing facility with technical vocabulary throughout their school years.

Getting Started

Here's what I do at the beginning of each school year to set the stage and put the process of vocabulary acquisition in forward motion.

Something to Write Home About

About two weeks before school begins, I send a letter to parents in which I describe the tools students need to have for math class and general information about plans for the year ahead (see Figure 1–1). After outlining the intended content for the year, I discuss the attention that will be directed to vocabulary and why, and I invite their involvement and support. (At the first parent meeting several weeks into the school year, I talk about this in more depth.) In the letter I also mention that they will have an opportunity to experience more math language during our FAMILY MATH series. (A feature of each strand-oriented evening event is a mathematics vocabulary "scavenger hunt." For example, during the "probability" FAMILY MATH night, parent/child partners look and listen for probability-related vocabulary as they explore the stations and participate in group games and analyses. Each family has a program sheet that has a place to record the words as they are found. At the close of the session, the partners who have recorded the most terms win a prize.)

The letter home is my initial proactive outreach. Decades of research have shown that the single most important factor in a child's academic achievement is parental involvement (Henderson and Berla 1994; Dykstra and Fege 1997; Down 1997). Because my approach to teaching mathematics is not "traditional," I feel I need to address the issue of public perception. I am not so naïve as to believe I am shielded from the achievement angst permeating the current educational climate. It is essential to be thoughtful about the beliefs and potential responses of parents and community members. Because they do not participate in the deliberate class discussions designed to foster attitude shifts, they especially need frequent communiqués about what we are doing and why.

Probably the most important way to communicate to parents is through the articulate voices of students who are learning mathematics deeply and confidently. Until those voices become a reality, frequent brief bulletins about classroom strategies, reasons for the strategies, and student work showing progress are in order. The important message I need to convey is that studying mathematics vocabulary is worthwhile and advantageous and that whatever

August 15, 2000

Dear Grades 7/8 Parents,

For seventh grade parents this is my first official contact as your child's math teacher and for eighth grade parents a continuing effort to keep everyone informed about planning and programming for the year ahead.

I'm working hard on this year's mathematics program, which will include rational numbers (including percents), algebra, similarity, integers, three-dimensional measurement, probability, and irrational numbers. Learning about and using the special vocabulary related to these mathematics topics will be a major element of our study. As the year begins please encourage your child to talk about her or his math vocabulary work. Every opportunity to use the language helps students develop deeper understanding of the mathematics and supports their ability to communicate their mathematical reasoning.

Organizational issues impact the materials and resources all students need to have. We will be using 1- or 1½-inch three-ring binders. We will organize the binders during our first session. Besides the usual three-ring paper and dividers, which CTL will provide, each student needs to have a math toolkit that can be easily stored in the binder. These are things you need to purchase and include:

A flexible container, such as a study zipper lock freezer bag, large enough to hold:
A combination 6 inch/15 centimeter ruler, a compass [drawing tool], a protractor, a small transparent tape dispenser, and reinforcements for the three-hole-punched paper.

In addition to the above purchased items, from time to time students will be asked to carry additional items for homework and extended assignments, such as dice, color tiles, color cubes, etc. Please keep that in mind as you and your child prepare the kit. It will also be helpful to include several pencils and an eraser.

I have something for parents to be thinking about. I will hold a FAMILY MATH series for the Junior High. (Very popular in the past with both students and parents!) This means parent-child partners coming together for 4–6 sessions (spread throughout the year) to work on math problems together. It is an opportunity for students to "teach" their parents about graphing calculators and other math tools new to parents as well as some mathematics language. The sessions are in the early evening from 6:00–8:00 P.M. Please be prepared to let me know what night of the week might work best for your family.

Thanks so much for being the wonderful supportive parents that you are. I look forward to exploring and learning powerful mathematics with your children.

Please feel free to contact me at any time.

Sincerely,
Miki

FIGURE 1–1   *August Letter to Parents Preparing for the Year Ahead*

strategies engage and support students in learning and using math vocabulary are appropriate courses of action for increasing mathematical competence. That is a key message for students and their families as well.

Here's how Kail Cadman, a parent, reacted to her seventh grader's involvement in my nontraditional, vocabulary-laden math class: "[This] has been a thorough approach for our son. He really understands the concepts and theories behind each problem; he is not simply memorizing and repeating. With this understanding, he is able to explain what he is doing and apply it to other types of problems."

Creating the Classroom Climate

I design the first three days of class to help students become independent learners and understand how they are responsible for their own learning. Each activity of these first days is relevant to the robust mathematics vocabulary students are expected to acquire and use throughout their studies. These activities introduce students to the expectations for interacting in and with the environment, their level of responsibility for it, and their responsibility to each other.

Each program element or tool is introduced with time for questions. I want everyone to understand what's expected, how to proceed, and why. At the same time I demonstrate the responsibility I have as a teacher for designing the management tools and academic environment that will support and sustain their efforts.

Day 1: "Expectations for Mathematics," Binder Organization, and Problem Exploration   The students gather in the lab, our middle-level math and science room. We begin by reviewing my Expectations for Mathematics handout, which lobbies for sense making, problem solving, a variety of work configurations, and a safe environment where students are respected for communicating their thinking about mathematics. It also describes homework, tools for studying mathematics, and the math strands. Each student receives a three-hole-punched copy. We carefully read, interpret, and discuss each element. The following excerpt represents the first time we read and talk about the key role that mathematics vocabulary will play in the year ahead:

Everyday that we have mathematics you are expected to reflect upon the work that you do and write about it in your math journal, which will be part of your binder. Developing your math vocabulary is very important to being able to communicate effectively in mathematics.

I explain that as their experience with vocabulary develops throughout the year, they will be creating their own personal collection of vocabulary terms they need to understand—five each week. I do not specify that students learn at least five *new* math words each week. Some of these words will be new, but not all will be. They are words students need to understand better. For example, one of the first words we encounter each year is *factor*. Students are usually familiar with the term as a number that is multiplied—a *multiplier* or a *multiplicand*. As we move through the year, they learn that the term also is applied to whole numbers that evenly divide a number; a divisor or quotient; the opposite of multiple; and the base in an exponential expression. And the use and meaning of the term continue to broaden in the algebra units.

When we finish reading and talking about expectations, the handout goes home for parents or guardians to read and sign. It is the first homework assignment of the year and is to be returned the following day.

We then move on to organize the student three-ring binders. Each student receives a copy (again three-hole punched) of the Binder Organization sheet (see Figure 1–2), a set of dividers, and a vocabulary word wall folder (described in detail later in this chapter).

◆ The first section of the student binder is the **journal,** where all work done during class is recorded. It is the original record of any vocabulary that we encounter during problem solving, minilessons with note taking, and daily reflections. Students get about a dozen sheets of lined three-ring-binder paper to start the journal.

◆ The **homework** section is for current assignments. Homework stays here until it is processed in class or submitted to me for review.

◆ The **forms and guides** section is home for the formal "rites and rules" of the classroom. For example, the Binder Organization sheet

BINDER ORGANIZATION

HOMEWORK LOG IS KEPT IN FRONT OF THE JOURNAL SECTION—
it is the first thing you see when you open your binder.

Dividers are organized in the following order:

- ◆ Journal
- ◆ Homework—where in-process and completed assignments are kept
  so you always know where your homework is
- ◆ Forms and Guides—where the Expectations handout, guidelines,
  rubrics, etc. are kept throughout the year
- ◆ Returns—where papers are kept until completion of the unit; then
  they go into the archives
- ◆ Vocabulary—word wall folder used as index and for submitting for
  evaluation
- ◆ MATHCOUNTS materials—where you keep warm-ups and
  workouts to use during downtime.

Student math textbooks are also kept in the binder, in the front.

FIGURE 1–2 *Binder Organization Guide for Students*

goes here, as does the Expectations for Mathematics handout when it is returned the following day (after the parent signature has been checked).

◆ The **returns** section is the interim archive for student work that has been reviewed by me and returned to the student. It is especially useful to the students when they're participating in the weekly vocabulary brainstorm, completing the biweekly self-evaluation, or preparing portfolios (details of these processes are described in later chapters).

◆ The **vocabulary** section is unique. It includes each student's personal vocabulary entries and an oaktag word wall on which these entries are indexed.

◆ The final section of the binder is for **MATHCOUNTS** materials. MATHCOUNTS is a national competitive problem-solving program accessible through the *<www.mathcounts.org>* website. An annual MATHCOUNTS School Handbook, containing ample problems for the academic year (along with their solutions), is provided free to every middle school in America, but a registration fee is required to participate in the competition. Solving the problems in this section is optional, but all students have the materials available to them. Included is an extensive vocabulary list provided by the program.

Then I distribute the homework log and describe how it is to be used. Everyone records the first homework assignment—taking home and returning the Expectations for Mathematics document—as I model on the overhead. The homework log goes *before* the binder tabs, so that it is the first thing in the binder.

From this point on students are responsible for replenishing (from the classroom paper shelf) the paper in their binders, as well as the homework log, as needed.

Once the binders are organized, there's just enough time to get started on the first problem of the year, which requires some investigation and introduces the format for writing about a problem-solving experience. (The process is detailed in Chapter 4.) Students are expected to explore possible solutions and record *all of their thinking and work* in their math journals. I have them begin immediately, working with a partner if they choose. I also ask them to spend a half hour on the problem for homework, record their progress, and be prepared to share their thinking. (This assignment is also recorded in the homework log.)

Day 2: Student Guidelines for Mathematics Journal and Binder, Problem-Solving Write-Up, and Resources Scavenger Hunt The second day starts with checking the returned Expectations handout—parent signature in place, and placing it in the forms and guides section of the binder. Then, before revisiting the problem, I distribute another handout, Student Guidelines for Mathematics Journal and Binder, which clarifies how the journal and overall binder will be used and maintained throughout the year. (These guidelines are detailed in Chapter 4, Problem-Solving Write-Ups, and Chapter 6, Expanding Vocabulary with Journals and Homework.) When we finish working with the document, it goes home for parents or guardians to read, sign, and return.

Now we return to the problem we started yesterday. The students share their thinking and talk about the work they've done so far. We note the various vocabulary terms that are useful in describing the explorations and findings, and finally I introduce the format for writing up a problem-solving experience. (The write-up process is detailed in Chapter 4.) The write-up becomes another homework assignment, this time long term. I model and check on the recording of this first long-term assignment in the homework log.

We finish off the second day with a "room resources" scavenger hunt. I hand out a list of all the tools and resources students will use in the math lab throughout the year. (The reference books, which include a variety of dictionaries, are especially important for vocabulary development.) I want every student to be clear about where these resources can be found and to where they must be returned after use. The listed resources and tools are organized on shelves throughout the room. I place NORTH, EAST, SOUTH, and WEST signs on the walls so that as pairs of students race around finding the individual items, they can easily design a way to record a location—a subtle mathematics-related language opportunity. (For example, "Compasses: west wall, left side, middle shelf, between rulers and tape.")

By the end of the second day students have a pretty good handle on the basics of organization and management. It's my first attempt to help everyone understand how to keep track of his or her mathematics work. As each day passes, there is constant reinforcement, and the tools and guidelines are easy to access and review when necessary.

Day 3: Math Survey On the third day the students bring back the Guidelines. (I am fortunate to have excellent support from the administration regarding homework. There are consequences for noncompliance, and I establish and reinforce the standards from the outset.) Once I check for parent signatures and record a completed assignment, the Guidelines also go into the forms and guides section of the student binder.

The remainder of the day is devoted to a homemade math survey covering all the math strands, with an emphasis on rational numbers. The major purpose of the survey is to give me specific information about my students' computational skill levels, and their perceptions of mathematics and mathematics vocabulary. I readminister the survey at the end of the year in order to stay informed about students' growth in understanding and competence.

In one section of the survey, I ask students to try to get inside my head and come up with reasons why I might want them to study vocabulary as part of math class. The students handle this task well, pretty much convincing themselves that mathematics vocabulary plays an important role in their mathematics work. Here are some representative responses:

- You need to know vocabulary. It's like knowing everyday words and what they mean.
- If you know about math vocabulary, then it helps to understand math better.
- It is easier to explain a problem if you have a good vocabulary.
- You need to know what different vocabulary words mean in order to know what a question means.
- You understand what you are doing if you know what the words mean.
- If you know that vocabulary, you can better express what you need to explain; it helps you grasp concepts if you know the vocabulary.
- If you understand math, you should be able to define the words you're using.
- To talk about mathematics and describe it, we need mathematics vocabulary.
- Math involves many unfamiliar words, and to fully understand mathematics one must learn them.
- Helping others to understand what you're trying to say, to understand what others are saying, to express your way of doing something more clearly.

- It helps reading textbooks and understanding basic math concepts and later on more difficult ones.

- It helps you converse and write down what you're trying to say to other people, and it helps you know more about mathematics and makes you look smarter.

- It helps explain your thinking and helps you understand other people's thinking.

- It helps us use specific terms and avoid the word *thing*.

- You can describe what you're trying to do with a problem to the rest of the world.

I also have students talk about how they define mathematics. Because most of their ideas relate to numbers or computing, I choose the word *mathematics* to kick off the vocabulary study for the year. We start by checking the entries in several dictionaries. The interesting and telling part of these dictionary descriptions is the etymological chain, tracing the development of the term from the Greek *mathēmatikos,* meaning "inclined to learn." Attached meanings include "pay attention to," "be alert, cheerful," "think," "the mind," and finally "what is learned." Nothing in the etymological transformation refers to numbers and ciphering!

It delights me to think, as the Greeks did, that mathematics is all about learning. Mathematics is about problem solving, collecting data, searching for relationships, and identifying patterns. Being able to communicate throughout these processes is a critical part of becoming skillful and competent mathematicians and expanding our knowledge.

Immersion and Subversion

Earlier in this chapter, I brought up Zal Usiskin's idea that "language immersion" is critical to learning mathematics. As if to underline its importance, when Camille Blachowicz and Peter Fisher (1996) summarize the research on vocabulary learning in general, they place immersion at the top of their list of seven characteristics essential for robust vocabulary development in any discipline:

1. Immerse students in words.
2. Encourage students to be active in making connections between words and experiences.
3. Encourage students to personalize word learning.
4. Build on multiple sources of information.
5. Help students control their learning.
6. Aid students in developing independent strategies.
7. Assist students in using words in meaningful ways; meaningful use leads to long-lasting learning. (7)

While immersion may be the ultimate goal, this book is filled with strategies that teachers can dip into and out of as it suits their needs. Elements can be easily added or refined each year, allowing an effective regimen to develop over time.

After years of such practice, the idea of vocabulary immersion is now an important part of my mathematics program. Students are immersed in mathematics vocabulary in all class work and homework: warm-ups, problems, investigations, explorations, assessments, recording, reporting, writing, speaking, and reading. Through example, demonstration, and direct instruction, students discover that a key element in their mathematical learning comes through the substantial use of technical vocabulary.

However, the vocabulary focus of my classroom is not an add-on to the curriculum, or *more* to teach; it is a *way* to teach mathematics. Learning and using mathematics vocabulary becomes part of the way we do business. Three levels of vocabulary work are represented throughout the program. I like to think of them as *doors, windows,* and *secret passageways.* A *door* is an obvious and direct strategy. Examples are the development of a personal mathematics vocabulary, and special writing assignments using unit-related collections of vocabulary terms. A *window* is a less obvious, but still visible strategy. For example, when we are ready to submit biweekly self-evaluations, I "sweep" the room, asking each student for a different concept he or she has been studying. While I record the terms on the whiteboard we're indirectly reviewing vocabulary. Or, after a class discussion and before students write a mathematical reflection or summary, we talk about words that will help do the job right. In contrast, *secret passageways* do not have an obvious vocabulary connection— rather, the connection is submerged, even subversive. Secret passageways are pervasive and subtle, built into the culture of journal entries, working with partners and small groups, and sharing strategies. Of course, each of these situations is also an opportunity for the meaningful use of technical mathematics terminology.

Part of establishing "vocabulary immersion" is having students think about what it means to "know" a word. Constructing word knowledge involves developing meaning over time through many rich encounters in a variety of contexts, and using a variety of strategies, ranging from incidental references to direct instruction. Vocabulary words need to be used deliberately and meaningfully, incorporating newly understood relationships as more sophisticated contexts unfold. For example, after we had discussed using the distributive property when multiplying multidigit numbers, especially during mental math warm-ups, Audrey transferred this understanding to the more complex context of multiplying a fraction and a mixed number (see Figure 1–3). She learned about the distributive property over time, in the context of the multiplication "facts," multidigit algorithms for multiplying and dividing whole numbers, and finally an algorithm for multiplying fractions.

Planning for Vocabulary Acquisition

Principles and Standards for School Mathematics (NCTM 2000) reminds teachers to honor the developmental approach to vocabulary acquisition:

> Beginning in the middle grades, students should understand the role of mathematical definitions and should use them in mathematics work. Doing so should become pervasive in high school. However, *it is important to avoid a premature rush to impose formal mathematical language;*

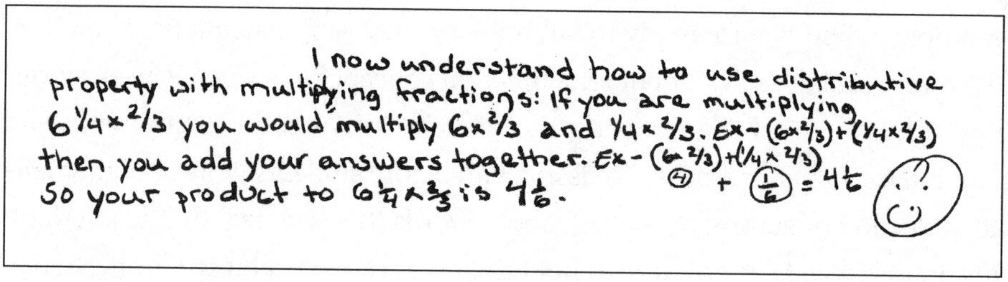
I now understand how to use distributive property with multiplying fractions: If you are multiplying $6\frac{1}{4} \times \frac{2}{3}$ you would multiply $6 \times \frac{2}{3}$ and $\frac{1}{4} \times \frac{2}{3}$. Ex- $(6 \times \frac{2}{3}) + (\frac{1}{4} \times \frac{2}{3})$ then you add your answers together. Ex- $(6 \times \frac{2}{3}) + (\frac{1}{4} \times \frac{2}{3})$ $4 + \frac{1}{6} = 4\frac{1}{6}$ So your product to $6\frac{1}{4} \times \frac{2}{3}$ is $4\frac{1}{6}$.

FIGURE 1–3 *Audrey's Description of Her Growing Understanding of the Distributive Property*

students need to develop an appreciation for the need for precise definitions and for the communicative power of conventional mathematical terms by first communicating in their own words. Allowing students to grapple with their ideas and develop their own informal means of expressing them can be an effective way to foster engagement and ownership. (63)

In order to "avoid a rush to premature formal math language," we always layer our vocabulary discussion by first using familiar language to describe mathematical situations. For example, students will describe a diagonal as something that goes across the middle of the figure. They then sketch visual examples and counterexamples while discussing and refining the definition. I remind them to strive for "elegance" in their description without leaving out new understanding. It's a first step in considering how much information is "necessary" to define a term, either formally or informally, as well as what is "sufficient"—having enough but not too much. Two important criteria established to support any level of vocabulary work are to always make sense and to search continuously for deeper conceptual understanding.

Using NCTM's Standards as a guide, I begin each unit with an informal assessment of where my students are in terms of their math language. We explore the following questions:

- What do we already know about this area of study?
- How are we currently using mathematical and nonmathematical terms to describe our related math thinking, our problem interpretations, and our solution processes?

◆ Where might we need to be more efficient and articulate in expressing our thinking more clearly?

The students search their collective backgrounds and experiences for familiar math language. Depending on the range and diversity of student backgrounds, a great deal of the work comes from peer contributions. For example, whenever we begin a study of the circumference and area of circles, the students collectively explain and record their definitions of a circle and their understanding of *diameter, radius, chord, formulas for circumference and area,* and *pi,* even though no one can explain the key relationships. Then I establish the students' current conceptual level based on how they use and explain the vocabulary they "know." This approach gives students a personal stake in adding depth to their knowledge and their ability to communicate mathematically. By recognizing the vocabulary that is already available to them, students are better attuned to a more useful term for any given concept when it appears. Once I understand where students are, we begin to work toward a higher level of understanding.

The vocabulary study in my classroom is always undertaken in the context of developing mathematical understanding—vocabulary is a tool for communicating and demonstrating understanding. And because understanding vocabulary is key to using it effectively, dictionary definitions are not a primary source. Hearing, seeing, and using the terminology in mathematical contexts comes first. These processes are essential to establishing personal ownership. Checking dictionary definitions then supports and clarifies developmental understanding. Similarly, none of the vocabulary terms we develop throughout the school year come from published lists; they are collections of terms encountered during our work in mathematics.

Students hear terms used in context. Then students use them during discussions and in their writing to describe the mathematics they're doing and learning about. Growth continues when students keep a written record of the words that they're learning and when they have frequent opportunities and reasons to use the vocabulary to communicate mathematically. Reading interesting stories, books, and articles about mathematics, mathematicians, and the work mathematicians do adds breadth to vocabulary acquisition and overall mathematical understanding. Finally, students' reflections on the progress they are making give them personal equity in the competent and confident use of the specialized language of mathematics.

Building a Personal Mathematics Vocabulary

Personal math vocabulary is an important part of each student's binder. The Guidelines handout discusses the role of vocabulary in mathematics work and lays out the details for a yearlong accumulation of mathematics vocabulary:

> Math vocabulary is the last section of your binder. We will develop this vocabulary as we explore and review the different areas of mathematics. Each entry should include a definition, as well as illustrations and/ or examples. Since your definitions may change over time as your understanding develops and expands, be sure to leave lots of space for each entry. Your personal "word wall" appears at the end of the vocabulary section and is an index of the vocabulary you know.

In class I explain that when new vocabulary emerges during class discussion, it will be announced as a "new collectible." That's a signal for them to jot it down in their journal, along with brief notes that attach meaning to the term or connect it to what we're studying. To encourage student reflection, I sometimes have students note in their journal words in each of the following categories:

- ◆ Mathematics words I am confident using.
- ◆ Mathematics words I understand but need to practice using.
- ◆ Mathematics words I don't understand or use.

Next, I tell students that we will devote the last portion of every Thursday's class period to group vocabulary brainstorming, maintaining a continuous list of terms on chart paper. (It's more efficient to update the list once a week rather than daily or each time a term is mentioned in class.) During the brainstorming session, each student is expected to scan his or her notes (and brain) for terms that are not already listed. The charted list of terms is a constant resource for the students that is always available.

I also explain that every Friday is "vocabulary day," the due date for a minimum of five new entries in each student's individual vocabulary record. Each student decides the specific terms that are most important to her or his individual mathematics development and understanding. Students must write the definitions in their own words based on what they understand about the term when they enter it. They are encouraged to consult mathematics and regular dictionaries, but the meaning they write must be in their own words and represent their own thinking. The illustration and/or example is a critical part of each entry.

At the beginning of Friday's class, each student shares one new entry, along with his or her definition for the term. No repeats are allowed. I or a student volunteer records each term on the whiteboard as it is announced, until no new terms can be contributed. (Sometimes a student will ask to re-peat a term because she has a different definition—this is certainly allowed, because it encourages the class to critique the definitions by analyzing the differences.) "Vocabulary day" is another excellent opportunity to hear and use the language of mathematics in a meaningful context. It is also a time to celebrate our growth by acknowledging the individual contributions of students.

Next, I explain that their personal word wall will become the foundation of their vocabulary collections. A classroom word wall is a display of the alphabet on large sheets of paper on which words may be listed under the letter with which they begin. I adapt it for individual use by printing a matrix of twelve evenly spaced rectangles on each side of a 12-by-18-inch piece of oaktag (for a total of twenty-four rectangles). Each rectangle has one letter printed in the upper-left-hand corner, with the exception that X, Y, Z, are together in the final rectangle. The sheet is then folded in half to make a 9-by-12-inch folder, and the folded edge is three-hole punched. On the first page are sections A–F, the second page, G–L, the third page, M–R, and finally S–Z. (See Figure 1–4.)

The five words chosen by each student each week are entered into the vocabulary section of her or his binder in the order in which they are chosen and are numbered continuously (the five words selected for the first week are numbered 1 through 5, the five words selected for the second week are

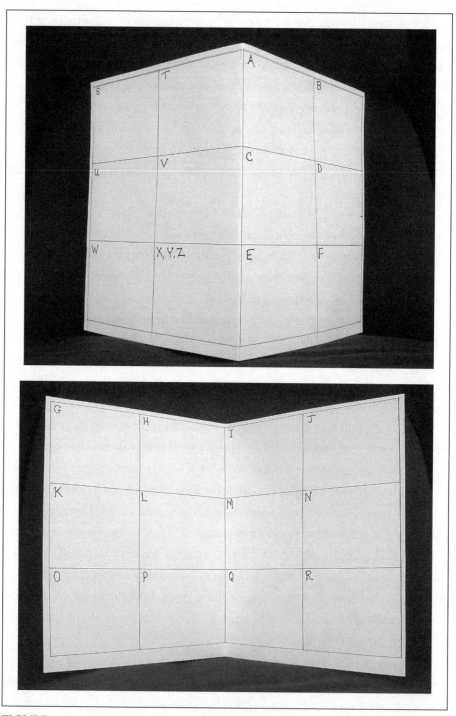

FIGURE 1–4 *Individual Student "Word/Wall" Made From 12 × 18 Oaktag; Side One Becomes the Outside of the Folder, Side Two Becomes the Inside of the Folder.* Set Photo by Donald Murray.

numbered 6 through 10, and so on). The word wall becomes an index of these terms—each one is recorded in the appropriately lettered section, followed by its entry number. This allows the students or me to locate an entry quickly and also avoids duplication of entries over the year. Figure 1–5a shows a page from a student's vocabulary section as indexed in her word wall folder. Figure 1–5b shows a typical accumulated list for an entire academic year. The vocabulary pages in Figure 1–6 illustrate the variety of definitions students develop. These definitions, along with the examples and illustrations, give me excellent insight into the level of student understanding. For example, when Brenna records her understanding of decimals, she relates decimal place value to the denominator of the equivalent common fraction. I now know more about the depth of her understanding of the number system as well as the confident connections she makes between different fraction representations.

At least once a month students submit their vocabulary entries and personal word wall for evaluation. Just before they do, they exchange them for a peer review, counting to see that the minimum number of entries are in place and checking for spelling as well as they are able. The results are imperfect but they take the job seriously, and I find it is time well spent.

When assessing these vocabulary materials I use a form that focuses separately on the word wall and on the vocabulary entries. On the word wall I'm looking for the number of terms entered, their spelling, and their overall legibility. (For example, on Ceysa's word wall I notice *communitive* rather than *commutative* properties. I underline these words *in pencil* so that her attention is drawn to the *need for correction.* I also talk with her about the root of the word being *commute* as a way to help her better understand the concept and how the term is used.) On the vocabulary entries I'm looking for definitions, spelling, examples and illustrations, and overall presentation. I also check to see that students are satisfying the requirements for continuously updating and correcting entries. The students become very attached to these vocabulary tools and often continue to use them in high school.

By developing their own personal vocabularies, the class develops vocabulary understanding in context. This helps us talk about the mathematics we're doing using more sophisticated language, language that is more direct and precise. Their developing vocabulary gives students a resource for alternate

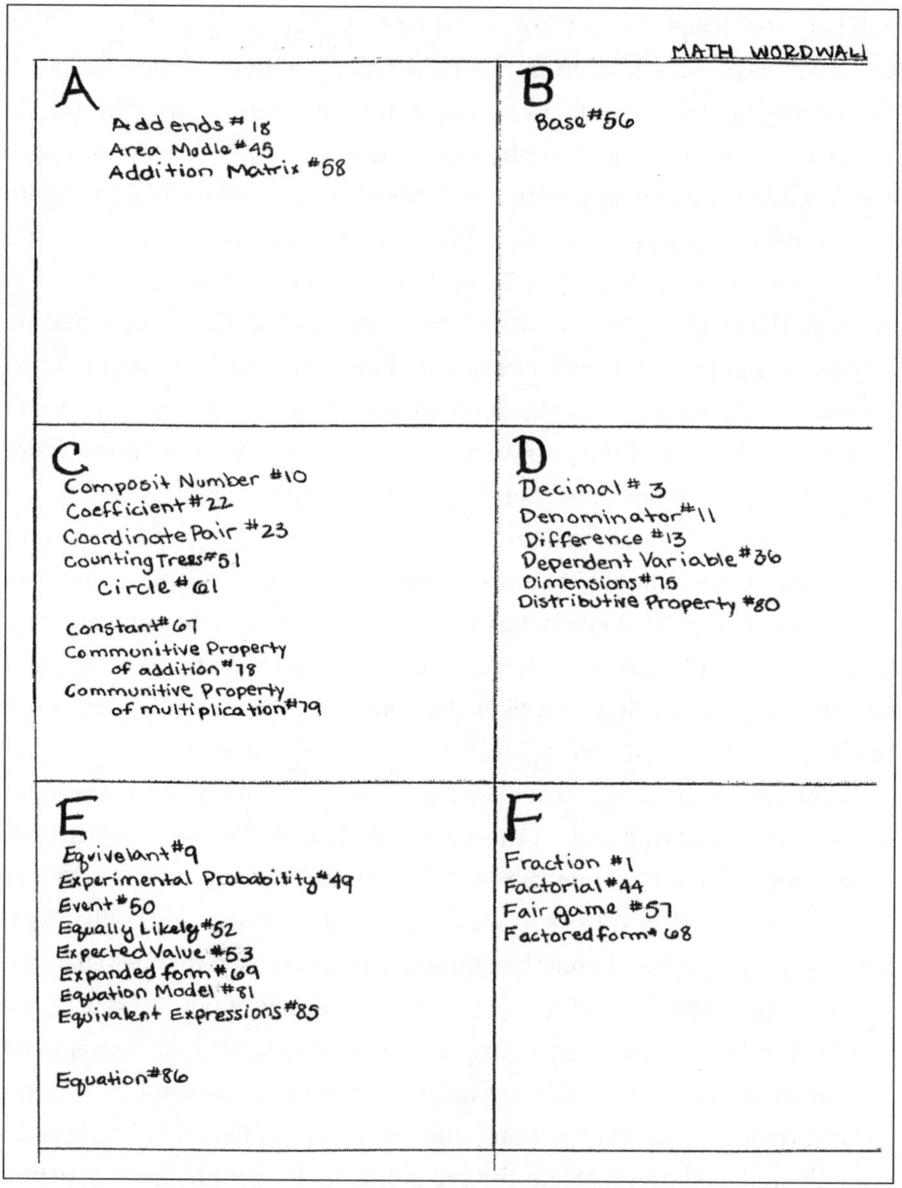

A
Addends #18
Area Modle #45
Addition Matrix #58

B
Base #56

C
Composit Number #10
Coefficient #22
Coordinate Pair #23
Counting Trees #51
    Circle #61

Constant #67
Communitive Property
    of addition #78
Communitive Property
    of multiplication #79

D
Decimal #3
Denominator #11
Difference #13
Dependent Variable #36
Dimensions #75
Distributive Property #80

E
Equivelant #9
Experimental Probability #49
Event #50
Equally Likely #52
Expected Value #53
Expanded form #69
Equation Model #81
Equivalent Expressions #85

Equation #86

F
Fraction #1
Factorial #44
Fair game #57
Factored form #68

FIGURE 1–5a   *The Front Cover of Ceysa's Word Wall and a Page From Her Personal Vocabulary Showing the Indexing of Entries 49–52*

Vocabulary 49-52

49. Experimental Probability- a probability that
    is obtained by experimentation.
    Ex: turn : 1 2 3 4 5   A=$^2/_5$ B=$^2/_5$
        outcome: A C B B A   C=$^1/_5$

50. Event- a set of outcomes.

51. Counting Tree- a diagram used to determin
    the probability and the number of possible
    outcomes.

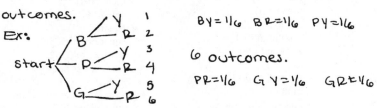

    BY=$^1/_6$ BR=$^1/_6$ PY=$^1/_6$

    6 outcomes.

    PR=$^1/_6$ GY=$^1/_6$ GR=$^1/_6$

52. Equally Likely- when two or more events
    have the same probability of being chosen.
    Ex: all of the outcomes in #51 are equally
    likely.

FIGURE 1–5a   *continued.*

A Typical Word List for One Academic Year

Key—Term (entry word number): Each word is followed by its numerical identification as an entry word in the student's personal vocabulary collection.

absolute value (64)
acute (109)
addends (62)
algorithm (108)
angle (60)
area (24)
bar graph (22)
bimodal (17)
categorical data (9)
census (130)
centimeter (32)
circle (47)
circumference (27)
coefficient (84)
commutative (65)
complementary angles (68)
computation (22)
coordinate (14)
coordinate grid (80)
coordinate pair (81)
data (10)
decimal fraction (100)
decimal number system (56)
denominator (75)
dependent variable (83)
diagram (33)
difference (90)
dividend (71)
divisor (72)
equation (79)
equivalent rate (118)
equivalent ratio (102)
estimate (28)
estimation (116)
exponent (30)
expression (77)
factor (48)
fraction (40)
frequency (20)
geometry (49)
greatest common factor (GCF) (57)
grid (13)
histogram (127)
horizontal (106)

independent variable (82)
integers (41)
interior angles (123)
inverse (61)
irrational number (124)
least common multiple (LCM) (56)
length (34)
line (54)
linear (23)
line plot (18)
line segment (59)
magnitude (13)
manipulating data (105)
maximum (36)
mean (8)
median (7)
meter (31)
minimal path (89)
minimum (37)
minuend (98)
mode (2)
multiplicand (4)
multiplier (3)
negative number (87)
number sentence (78)
numerical data (10)
obtuse (110)
opposites (63)
outlier (43)
palidrome (26)
parallel lines (66)
parallelogram (91)
part-to-part ratio (103)
part-to-whole ratio (104)
pentomino (36)
percentage (99)
perimeter (25)
pi (58)
point (52)
polygon (53)
population density (125)
positive number (88)
precise (29)
prime factorization (41)

prime number (46)
prime division (47)
product (6)
quadrant (85)
quadrilateral (86)
quantity (5)
quotient (73)
range (1)
rate (111)
rate table (120)
ratio (117)
rectangle (39)
reciprocal (96)
remainder (114)
rhombus (45)
sampling (120)
scale (101)
square (51)
squared (21)
square root (135)
square unit (132)
stacked bar graph (119)
statistics (165)
stem-and-leaf plot (128)
subtrahend (97)
sum (30)
supplementary angles (67)
symbolic method (133)
table (134)
trapezoid (95)
transversal (67)
triangle (55)
two-dimensional (70)
unit (131)
unit rate (115)
variable (76)
Venn diagram (121)
vertex (126)
vertical (107)
weight (113)
width (35)
x-axis (11)
y-axis (12)

FIGURE 1–5b   *A Sample Student Word List for an Entire Academic Year*

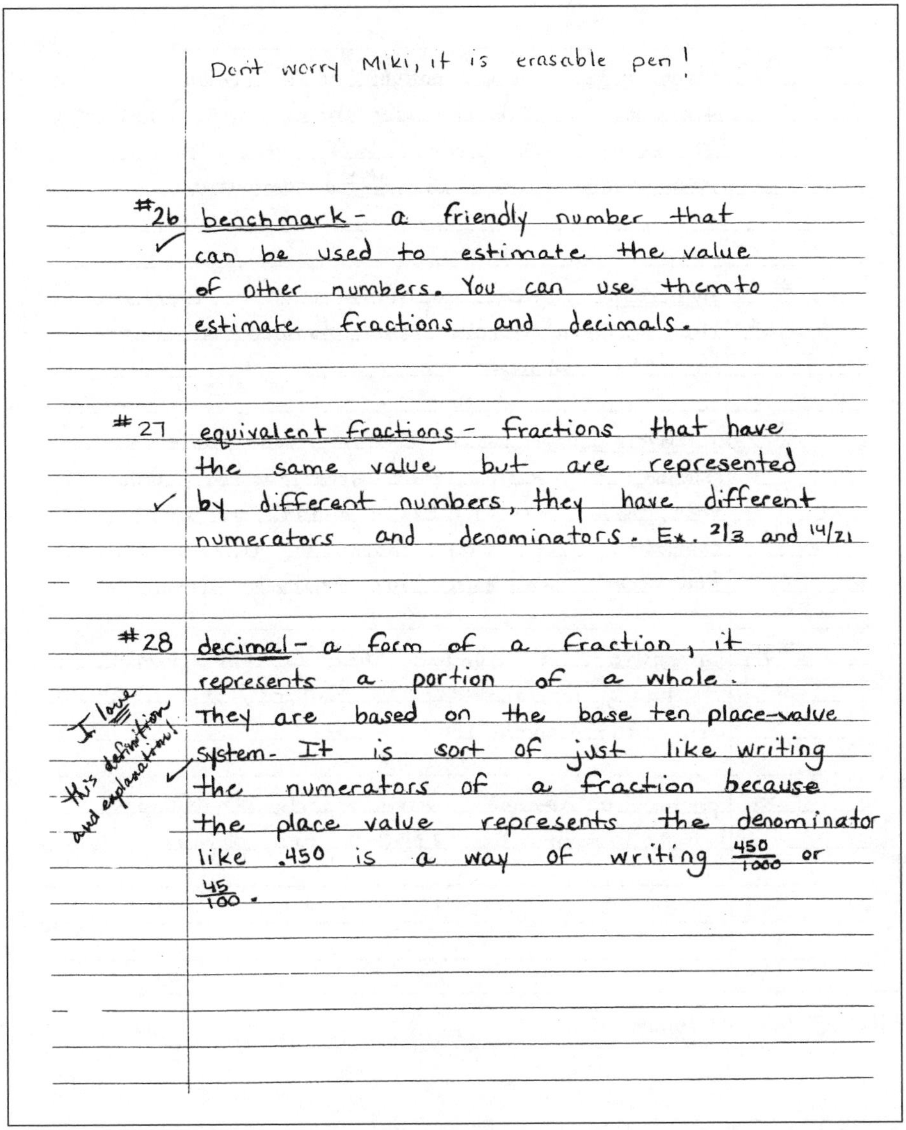

Don't worry Miki, it is erasable pen!

#26 benchmark - a friendly number that ✓ can be used to estimate the value of other numbers. You can use them to estimate fractions and decimals.

#27 equivalent fractions - fractions that have the same value but are represented ✓ by different numbers, they have different numerators and denominators. Ex. $\frac{2}{3}$ and $\frac{14}{21}$

#28 decimal - a form of a fraction, it represents a portion of a whole. *I love this definition and explanation!* They are based on the base ten place-value system. It is sort of just like writing the numerators of a fraction because the place value represents the denominator like .450 is a way of writing $\frac{450}{1000}$ or $\frac{45}{100}$.

FIGURE 1–6 *Two Pages From Brenna's Personal Vocabulary Illustrating Her Individually Developed Definitions and Examples*

```
#29   denominator - the bottom number in a
   ✓  fraction, the denominator shows the number
      of equal size pieces the whole has
      been made into. Ex. 3/4 - denominator


#30   numerator - the top number in a fraction,
   ✓  the numerator tells the number of parts
      in the whole.


#31   relatively prime - when numbers are prime in
      relation to each other, when the only factor
      they share is 1. Ex. 8 and 9 are both
      composite, but they share no factors other
      than one, so they are relatively prime.


#32   composite - a number that is not prime:
      it has 3 or more 1 factors. Ex. 4,6,8,9,10
      are all composite.


#33   prime - a number with exactly 2 factors;
      1 and itself. Ex. 2,3,5,7,11 are prime.
```

FIGURE 1–6   *continued.*

ways to describe a mathematical situation or offer another way to explain a solution. As a teacher, I'm now more comfortable asking students for other ways of stating problems, conjectures, patterns, or solutions—the heart of our classroom discourse. It's doable because they have the tools.

CHAPTER 2

Speaking Mathematics

It boils down to this—if you can't talk about math, you are unlikely to do it well.

—PAT WINGERT (1996, 96)

In my earliest attempts to incorporate vocabulary into the business of math class, I relied solely on having students talk through their practice and daily lessons. With younger students, even if it was only column addition, we focused on attaching the appropriate math name to each element. We used terms like *addends, sum, ones, tens,* and *hundreds,* made sure we read the numbers correctly, and renamed place values ("in the number 240, 24 tens equals 2 hundreds and 4 tens"). We explored partial sums and the commutative and associative properties to confirm the accuracy of computation.

As I learned about ways to vary the "speaking mathematics" format, my classroom repertoire of strategies grew. Today, speaking mathematics is only one of the techniques used in my math language immersion, but it still plays a key role in providing meaningful practice for improving and enhancing vocabulary.

The Full Spectrum of Talk

Noisy chatter, rigid silence, or something in between? A gathering of young people, especially middle school children, naturally lends itself to noisy chatter. For a stunning contrast in silence, begin math class by asking, "What is the meaning of pi and where does it come from?" No hands are raised and eyes glaze over or roll with avoidance.

Silence is good when it represents thoughtful reflection. Noisy chatter can be productive when engaged in to investigate problems, talk about interpretations or solutions, or prepare a response to a challenging question. Imagine the transformation after being instructed to talk with a partner or table group about a math question: The noise level ratchets up as the children move from *think* to *pair* and get ready to *share*. These three important phases are discussed in this chapter.

In my math classes I look to balance the positive silence (*think* time) and clamor (intense argumentation) with many midrange opportunities for productive mathematics discourse. NCTM's *Professional Standards for Teaching Mathematics* (1991) defines classroom discourse as "ways of representing, thinking, talking, agreeing, and disagreeing" (34) about what is mathematically reasonable, and how someone can go about determining that a particular idea makes sense. These characteristics of discourse are basic elements of our conversations.

Years ago, while attending a professional workshop, I learned that in order for a vocabulary word to become part of one's personal repertoire, it must be used in meaningful ways close to thirty times. The implications for mathematics vocabulary acquisition are daunting. A sizable percentage of this vocabulary is new to the students, and in many instances familiar terms take on new, very specific meanings in mathematics. For example, the word *relation* is not new for middle or high school students, but its mathematical meaning, *a set of ordered pairs,* is rigid and focused, in contrast to the dozen different ways the term might be used in casual conversation. I have as many as twenty-five fledgling mathematicians who need to use mathematics terms correctly and hear them used correctly. That means my classroom has to include as much focused talk about mathematics as I can generate so that students can come to own the language.

Stimulating Mathematics Conversations

Solving Problems

There's simply nothing like a good problem for generating classroom conversations. A good problem engages everyone and is a first-class motivator. The scenario goes something like this:

- ◆ Initial discussion centers on defining the problem; students are invited to share their interpretations.
- ◆ Next, pairs or small groups of three or four students work collaboratively to solve the problem.
- ◆ Groups or partners then present their solutions, as the rest of the class listens, asks questions, and finally summarizes what's been learned.

Played out, this simple scenario is rich with the language of mathematics and a treasure trove for vocabulary development. Consider the following simply stated problem:

How many natural-number factors does N have if $N = 2^3 \cdot 3^2 \cdot 5^1$? (2002–2003 MATHCOUNTS School Handbook, 51)

First I read the problem aloud to reinforce the language of exponents. A student asks if he can read it a different way. By the end of both readings we've heard the terms *to the third power, to the second power, to the first power, cubed,* and *squared.* Another student asks what a natural number is. Classmates respond:

"All whole numbers except zero."

"The same as counting numbers."

"One, two, three, and so on" (this boy goes to the whiteboard to write them in set notation—{1,2,3, . . .}).

With that clarification, I ask: "What's the math term that describes how N is expressed in the problem?" Responses include: "Using exponents."

"Also prime factors." "Prime factorization."

I then ask what the problem is asking them to do. Student responses include:

"To find the natural-number factors of N."

"I think we have to find the *number* of factors, not the factors."

"But I need to find the factors in order to find the number of factors."

Once the students have demonstrated that they understand the problem, they begin the second phase—*pair*—solving it collaboratively. I add that once they have a solution, they need to think about whether there might be a more efficient solution. I hint that there may be a reason that N is expressed with its prime factorization in exponential form. If they're unclear about what *prime factorization* or *exponential form* is, they need to talk about it with their group.

While the students are working, I visit groups, mostly listening to conversations, occasionally asking questions to redirect or support. Here's some of the conversation I hear:

"I've got it . . . N is equal to 360."

"How do you know?"

"Two to the third power is eight, and three squared is nine, and five to the first power is just five, so I multiplied them. Hey, you know every number to the zero power is one, that's so weird."

"There must be an easier way; exponential form has something to do with it. Oh no, maybe it's the prime numbers."

"I listed all the factor pairs and I know there are twenty-four."

"What do you mean by *factor pairs*? I get twenty-eight."

"I tested each number by dividing with the calculator."

And so on.

Time for the third phase, *sharing*. A group lists twelve factor pairs for 360 in an organized column on the whiteboard to support their solution of twenty-four natural-number factors. They also explain why N is 360. The student with twenty-eight factors objects and says that they are missing the factor 16. Other students check with calculators to convince him that 16 is not a factor. One student points out that 16 couldn't be a factor because 16 is equal to 2 to the fourth power and there aren't four 2s in the prime factorization. Another group presents their "much more efficient" solution. They evaluated each prime factor: 2 to the third power is 8 and 8 has four factors; 3 squared is 9 and 9 has three factors; 5 to the first power is 5 and 5 has two factors. Multiplying 4 [factors] × 3 [factors] × 2 [factors] = 24. They knew twenty-four was correct, because listing all the factors also gave them twenty-four.

Now we have a new conjecture: Does this work for all numbers? And finally, how does the number of factors for each prime number relate to its exponent, leading to the number of "powers" of each prime (including the zero power!).

There's still more work to do with this problem, such as relating each natural-number factor to the prime factorization and understanding why the numbers of factors for the prime numbers were multiplied. But we stop here and will revisit the topic later. Students have bumped into important mathematical ideas but most important is the rich use of vocabulary. We've had a lively twenty minutes of highly focused mathematical conversation, using technical terminology in meaningful ways in the context of a simply stated problem.

The context of a good problem provides several opportunities for using vocabulary meaningfully. Each of these opportunities is evident in the group problem-solving scenario illustrated above. They include:

◆ Describing the problem (evident when the class is defining the problem).

◆ Describing one's thinking about the problem (evident during problem clarification, small-group work, and class discussion and summary).

- Exploring possible solution strategies or explaining and justifying various algorithms (evident during small-group work and whole-group sharing).
- Sharing, explaining, and presenting arguments to justify a solution or solutions (evident during whole-group sharing and summarizing).

It is essential that selected or adapted problems lead to important mathematics as well as vocabulary, mathematics that is part of a well-organized, carefully sequenced curriculum. Today's standards-based curriculums are problem based and serve the purpose well. (Examples of standards-based middle school programs include *Connected Mathematics*, MATHThematics, *Math in Context*, and *MathScape*; K–5 examples include *Everyday Mathematics* and *Investigations*. Each of these programs was developed through NSF funding.) Additional problem resources that easily align with standards-based curriculums are:

- *Good Questions for Math Teaching*, 2002, by Peter Sullivan and Pat Lilburn.
- *MATHCOUNTS*, an annual collection of challenging problems like the example in the scenario above (*MATHCOUNTS* Foundation, 2002; website: *www.mathcounts.org*; email address: *mathcounts@nspe.org*).
- *50 Problem-Solving Lessons* (Math Solutions 1996), by Marilyn Burns.
- The centerfold Menu of Problems in NCTM's monthly *Mathematics Teaching in the Middle School*.

Good Questions for Math Teaching is especially helpful as a how-to guide for creating and implementing good problems to serve all curricular strands in any standards curriculum.

Asking Questions

Using questions (not in their problem-posing sense, but as they support exploring, probing, sharing, and discussing in the classroom) to promote vocabulary development tends to be a subversive technique. Questioning can bring about powerful classroom discourse while students are exchanging or preparing to exchange ideas. Being able to ask just the right question in an infinite set of circumstances is a substantial challenge for most teachers. Developing the fine art of questioning takes planning, practice, reflection, and persistence. Coming up with questions that will push students to discover concepts and learn the related vocabulary demands even more of a teacher. There are resources to help.

Literally hundreds of articles and books have been written about developing effective questioning techniques. Three of my favorites are:

◆ Stenmark, *Mathematics Assessment: Myths, Models, Good Questions, and Practical Suggestions* (NCTM 1991)

◆ Burns et al., *A Collection of Math Lessons Grades 1–3* (Math Solutions 1988); *Grades 3–6* (1987); *Grades 6–8* (1990)

◆ Coates et al., new FAMILY MATH II (EQUALS 2003)

Mathematics Assessment is a source for questions geared to specific purposes—problem comprehension, relationships, mathematical learning (31–32). The Math Solutions books embed the questions in transcripts of classroom lessons. *FAMILY MATH II* has a straightforward list of good questions to promote mathematical thinking along with useful advice about asking questions designed for use by teachers and parents (4, 5). However, I have found no list of questions to help me generate vocabulary-rich conversations. So I stumble along with a clear goal on a fuzzy pathway.

Here are some techniques for creating questions that will encourage vocabulary use:

◆ *Include the concept or target vocabulary as part of the question.* "What does it mean to talk about *corresponding* parts?" opens the door for responses that will include multiple uses of *corresponding* and *corresponds to* as students discuss the relationships between, and characteristics of, similar or congruent figures.

◆ *Ask for an explanation.* "How does this algorithm work?" may elicit a variety of responses, depending on the context (perhaps a student has designed an unorthodox algorithm for subtracting integers or whole numbers). Whatever the context, the question needs to be sincere.

◆ *Ask for a justification of a conjecture.* For example, after a student has used *cross-multiplication* to compare two fractions, asking "Why does this work?" or "Can you explain that another way?" encourages him to use mathematics vocabulary as part of his representation or argument.

Remember that some of the vocabulary will be used in the students' heads as they think about and reason out their responses (the fancy term for this is *metacognition*). This is why questioning is such a subversive technique for getting at vocabulary. Observers don't see or hear this usage, but *thinking* is done with language just as much as speaking and writing are. I want students to be aware of their own thinking and reasoning about mathematics.

During an exploration of the "Pirating Pizza" problem (*Connected Mathematics*, Bits and Pieces II) (see Figure 2–1), I gave one group member a five-by-eight-inch card with the following questions to help her keep everyone thinking about what they were doing and why:

◆ Before we go on, are we sure we understand this?

◆ What are our options?

◆ Do we have a plan?

◆ Are we making progress or should we reconsider what we are doing?

◆ Why do we think this is true? (NCTM 2000, 55)

When all the groups had finished, they shared their strategies, which I summarized on chart paper. (See Figure 2–2.) I then used the following questions to help them share and summarize:

Pirating Pizza

In this problem, you can use what you have discovered about adding and subtracting fractions to make sense of the havoc that the infamous Pizza Pirate is causing! As you work on the problem, look for patterns that can help you to solve it.

Problem 4.3

Courtney's class made a gigantic square pizza for a class party to be held the day after the final exam. They made it a week before the party so they would have time to study. To keep the pizza fresh, they stored it in the cafeteria freezer.

Unfortunately, the notorious Pizza Pirate was lurking in the area. That night, the Pizza Pirate disguised himself as a janitor, tiptoed into the cafeteria, and gobbled down half of the pizza! On the second night, he ate half of what was left of the pizza. Each night after that, he crept in and ate half of the pizza that remained.

After the final exam, Courtney's class went to get their pizza to start their celebration—and were stunned by what they found!

What fraction of the pizza was left for the party?

To help you answer this question, make a table or chart showing

- the fraction of the pizza the Pizza Pirate ate each day
- the fraction of the pizza he had eaten so far at the end of each day
- the fraction of the pizza that remained at the end of each day

Write a summary of how your group solved this problem. Draw any diagrams that will help you to show your thinking.

FIGURE 2–1 *Investigation 4 Problem 4.3 Pirating Pizza, From the Bits and Pieces II Unit of* Connected Mathematics *Series*

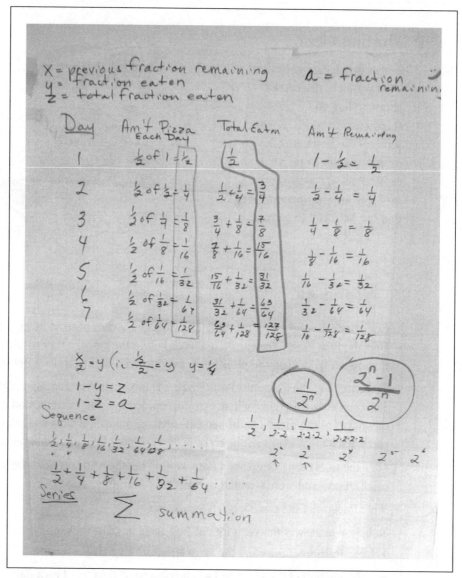

FIGURE 2–2 *Chart Paper Record of the Class Conversation Summarizing Pirating Pizza*. Set Photo by Donald Murray.

◆ Does anyone think differently? Why?

◆ What do you think will happen next?

◆ Is there a pattern, and, if so, how would you describe it?

◆ Why does this work?

It was one of the richest discussions ever to occur in any classroom of mine. The pattern question was especially productive: Students moved from "multiplying by two" to "powers of two for the denominators" and eventually attempted to generalize using the language of algebra. Then students had questions about connections they noticed between this and other problems from their collective pasts, bringing out the terms *sequence* and *series* and using the *summation symbol.* Several students got out math references and dictionaries to check on meanings and relate the terms to our data.

Another generic question for generating discourse about certain types of problems involving algorithms or generalizing rules from patterns is, "Is this always true, sometimes true, or never true, and why?" For example, when my students design "rules" for adding and subtracting integers, using this question to test their statements never fails to create a dizzying conversation. (See Chapter 5, Mathematical Reflections.)

During any problem postmortem, it's natural for students to begin asking questions. That's a thumbs-up event: You *want* them to ask good questions—of you, of each other, and of themselves. Posting a list of helpful generic questions that can be adapted to different content and discussion formats encourages them to do so. Here are some starters, and your students can add to the list:

- ◆ How did you know to try that strategy?
- ◆ What other examples did you test?
- ◆ Could you explain what you mean by . . . ?
- ◆ How do you know you have a solution?
- ◆ How is your solution like or different from the others?
- ◆ Is there another explanation?
- ◆ How did you figure that out?

Any of these questions from one student to others initiates a mathematical conversation and another opportunity to practice using vocabulary to communicate mathematically.

Using Literature

Reading a newspaper, magazine, or professional article is another way to stimulate good class conversation that involves mathematics. For example, some years ago I came across an entertaining article in the *New York Times* (see Figure 2–3) bemoaning what inflation has done to our concept of a million dollars. I make a copy of the article for each of my seventh and eighth graders, and we read it together, highlighting vocabulary and other mathematical issues. Inevitably, the article generates an intense discussion about *place value* and *scientific notation*. In the course of it we are driven to use all manner of mathematics vocabulary, and some misconceptions are revealed. Developmental gaps in student understanding emerge, particularly relevant to number sense. For example, students are unable to talk about the number of millions in a billion or describe the pattern of "periods" in large numbers. They are also unable to describe other place value relationships, such as how many thousands or ten thousands equal one million. Most are uncomfortable reading large numbers and are unable to do so accurately.

In response, we build a model of a million using base-ten blocks with these configurations (*unit cubes* = ones, *longs* = tens, *flats* = hundreds, and *large cubes* = one thousands) and meter sticks. Students predict how the model of a billion would compare in real-world dimensions. We talk about what each configuration of blocks represents and note each period pattern as it relates to the shape of the configuration. What place values are represented by cubes? What place values are represented by long rectangular prisms, and what place values have flat square prisms as models? In particular, what special kind of number is represented by the cube, what special kind of number is represented by the flat square, and how do you know? An important part of the discussion is summarizing new insights they have about their number system and the relative sizes of numbers.

Literature affords many opportunities to practice vocabulary:

◆ *Reading math poetry, stories, or articles.* In the example above, math vocabulary is used twice, once during the shared reading and again during the conversation about the reading. Students performing poems

A Billion, A Trillion, Whatever

By MICHAEL T. KAUFMAN

THE concept of a trillion has shifted in recent weeks from a fuzzy, imprecise and somewhat abstract notion into a hard-edged number like, say, 47 or 254 or 7,453.

Indeed, because of the Long-Term Capital Management fiasco, trillion has become the next big thing. (Of course, the Federal budget passed $1 trillion several years ago, but nobody pays attention to it.)

Before this recent shift in consciousness, a trillion, at least in everyday usage, was an expression more akin to zillion, gazillion and jillion. It was a way of connoting scads, heaps, plenitude and humongosity. In this it was like a light year. No one ever experienced a light year and no one ever saw a trillion anything. It was a poetic concept like all the stars in the heavens and all the grains of sand on the beaches.

But when Long-Term Capital Management's troubles became newsworthy in early October, it was reported that the firm had entered into "exotic financial transactions" valued at $1.25 trillion. Derivatives and forward contracts might not be universally comprehensible, but the basic image conveyed by the news stories was not at all meant as an abstract concept, like stars in the Milky Way. Anyone who plays poker could understand it; a group of people, a very finite group of people, were sitting around a table and making bets trying to win a pot worth $1.25 trillion, a figure even more impressive when it is represented like this: $1,250,000,000,000. That is quite real. It is so real it is scary.

For perspective, it may be useful to note that if somebody wanted to distribute $1 trillion equally among all 240 million Americans, he would have to dispense more than $4,000 to every man, woman and child.

Putting a dollar sign in front of very big numbers tends to make them real, though this does not always work for other units of wealth. For example, one can go to the Numismatic Museum in upper Manhattan and gaze at the quintillion pengo note that circulated in Hungary during a period of hyperinflation after World War II. Despite it's 18 zeros, 6 more than those of a trillion, it is not really awe inspiring. Even in the heyday of the pengo, one probably couldn't get much for a trillion, or quartillion or quintillion of them.

Devaluing the Millionaire

But there is a lesson here. Dollars, like pengos, fluctuate over time. And just as there are forces of inflation and devaluation affecting currencies, so there are semantic shifts in the numbers that come to be associated with money. Take millions and billions, which were as mythical as trillions were before Long-Term Capital helped make them a household concept.

There was a time when a million dollars was a pretty high standard. Telling somebody they looked like a million was considered a high compliment. Similarly, a millionaire was a rare species, generally depicted in cartoons as a cigar-smoking person in a top hat. Now, according to "The Millionaire Next Door," a best seller since it appeared in 1997, there are 3.5 million of them. That's 3,500,000, households. Though this is not exactly a dime a dozen, it is not one in a million either.

And within the last decade, some people began to be designated as billionaires. This has led to some confusion between the categories, notably the assumption that millionaires and billionaires are related subspecies who graze together. This is a fallacy that may be made clear by the following facts: A person with the net worth of $1 is closer in wealth to a person with a net worth of $50 million than the person with $50 million is to the person with $1 billion. Much, much closer. After all, the person with $1 is only $49,999,999 behind the millionaire, while the millionaire is $950,000,000 behind the billionaire.

This co-mingling of truly fat cats and the merely plump has long bothered John Allen Paulos, a Temple University mathematician who has written entertainingly about mathematics in everyday life. He advocates using scientific notation to describe the rich. For example, instead of the indistinct millionaire or multimillionaire, which could mean anyone who possessed more than a million or less than a billion (which the British refer to quite correctly as a thousand million) Mr. Paulos thinks exponents would help put the very rich in their appropriate places. For example, if one were to read about a 6×10^7 centerfielder, one could immediately determine that this was a $60 million variety of millionaire. A 3×10^6 adolescent baby sitter would be established a $3 million member of the phylum. And so forth.

Greater precision could also be achieved by borrowing from Indian usage. Indians, who number at least 8×10^8, have an increasingly useful word — crore — which means 10 million. And should the time come when the currently awesome trillion turns out to be small potatoes, there is the googol, which is the number 1 followed by 100 zeros, or 10^{100}. And if that's not enough, there is the googolplex which is 10 to the power googol.

FIGURE 2–3 New York Times *Article Used to Stimulate Class Conversation Around Place Value and Scientific Notation*

FIGURE 2–3   *continued.*

from Theoni Pappas's *Math Talk: Mathematical Ideas in Poems for Two Voices* (1991) have two additional opportunities: while researching the topic of the poem, either in order to introduce it or get ready to respond to questions about it, and while rehearsing their reading.

◆ *Performing skits that involve mathematical ideas.* Books such as *Anno's Mysterious Multiplying Jar* (Anno 1983) or the mathematical adventures of Robert in *The Number Devil* (Enzensberger 1998) motivate some students to act out mathematical ideas for younger students or their classmates, in the process encountering interesting vocabulary connected to concepts like factorials, number patterns, exponential growth, and square roots.

I'm always on the lookout for good pieces of literature that will stimulate students to talk math. Excerpts from professional journals are another good source. For example, my students are intrigued by and attentive to any articles about "brain research" related to math learning, because they can personalize it easily.

Conversation Groupings

Pairs

As the previous examples make clear, many math class conversations take place when partners are working together on some sort of challenge. Working in pairs allows the most voices to be heard—at least half of the students can be talking at one time. Obviously, such a classroom is not a quiet place. The teacher has to direct, monitor, and encourage the focus to remain on mathematics and its language.

"Build a Structure" is a specific partner activity, the goal of which is to encourage mathematics communication related to geometry. The activity was designed to be used with Geoblocks because of the variety of shapes within a set. However, it can also be done with other variably shaped sets of blocks, if you include a rule that color names can not be part of the conversation.

The students work in pairs, with each having the same four blocks. Place a barrier between each pair (such as an upright file folder). One person builds a structure with her blocks. She then tells her partner how to build the same structure without watching.

cription and construction of the structure is complete,
res. Are they the same? If not, where was the mis-
? How could it have been avoided? If you like: Have
tch roles.

Math for Girls and Other Problem Solvers (1981)
—*Diane Downie, Twila Slesnick, and Jean Kerr Stenmark*

why students are using a particular solution strategy can help
rify their thinking. For example, when partners are performing an
nent involving bouncing a ball from different heights, I ask them how
are recording their data and what they will do with the data once they
have it, prompting them to realize that if they organize their data in table
form it will be easier to analyze.

Suggesting that students identify more specific mathematical elements
in their solution strategies, or mentioning connections to math work done
previously, helps students prepare their results for sharing and keeps the
conversation focused on mathematics. For example, I ask pairs of students
to enter sets of equations (four in each set) in their graphing calculators and
compare the resulting graphs: how are the graphs alike, how are they different, and why? When students are stymied, I suggest they look for common elements and differences in the *equations* as well as in the graphs. I also
remind them of their previous work with coefficients.

My students understand that both partners are expected to share
their ideas during the whole-class discussion. This encourages individual
involvement while also giving a dominant partner the opportunity to do
some coaching. For example, Marcia and Jesse use mirrors to measure
the height of the ceiling indirectly. Marcia helps Jesse record the data,
work through the computations using similar triangles, and review how
the measurements were done. Marcia then sketches similar right triangles and asks Jesse to enter the known measurements and indicate
what the legs of the right triangles represent. Finally, Marcia explains
how to find the scale factor of the large triangle in relation to the small
one. They're ready to contribute their work to the class data and justify
their results.

Small Groups

Another common setting for classroom conversations is small groups. The distinct advantage of having three or four students engaged in an investigation is that there are more voices to listen to and learn from.

Cooperative learning problems are an excellent strategy for encouraging vocabulary use as well as a tool to help students learn about working effectively in small groups. My favorite cooperative problems are in Tim Erickson's *Get It Together* (1989). Four to six clues for each problem are stored in an envelope. The clues are passed out to members of the group. (If there are more clues than members, some members receive more than one clue.) The rules are very specific. Each member may look only at his or her own clue(s) and may not show them to anyone else. Members share their clues with the group orally. If everyone in the group has the same question, they may raise their hands and receive help from the teacher. (No answers are provided, even for teachers; students know when they have a solution or solutions.)

I post and review the following behavioral norms for cooperative learning problems:

- ◆ Follow the rules of the activity.
- ◆ Make sure everybody gets to participate.
- ◆ Listen to what other people say.
- ◆ Try to give reasons for what you say.
- ◆ Ask others for their opinions.
- ◆ Help others—without telling them what to do or giving them answers.
- ◆ Get help if you need it—from your group first. (Erickson, 10)

Figure 2–4 is an example of a cooperative learning problem from the number strand. Students working together on this problem encounter the following vocabulary, who knows how many times: *palindrome, digits, prime,*

Alexander's Number

Alexander's number is a palindrome, and the second and third digits are different.

Help your group find out what Alexander's number could be.

Alexander's Number

Alexander's number is prime and it's greater than one hundred.

Help your group find out what Alexander's number could be.

Alexander's Number

Alexander's number is odd, and the difference between the largest digit and the smallest digit is five.

Help your group find out what Alexander's number could be.

Alexander's Number

Alexander's number is less than one thousand, and the sum of its digits is 14.

Help your group find out what Alexander's number could be.

Alexander's Number

Alexander's number is not divisible by three, and it is less than 500.

Help your group find out what Alexander's number could be.

Alexander's Number

Alexander's number is a whole number with only two divisors: itself and one.

Help your group find out what Alexander's number could be.

FIGURE 2–4 *Alexander's Number From Tim Erikson's* Get It Together: *An Example of a Cooperative Learning Problem That Encourages and Depends on Vocabulary Growth*

odd, difference, less than, more than, sum, divisible, divisor, whole number, greater than, hundred, and *thousand.*

After each cooperative problem-solving session, we do a sweep around the room in which each student shares a mathematics term she or he has used. This provides reinforcement and closure. When small groups solve any kind of problem together, a spokesperson presents a group's solution to the class. This is another excellent opportunity to use math vocabulary, paying dividends for the speakers as well as the listeners.

In the problem in Figure 2–5, which is from *Connected Mathematics*, *Bits and Pieces II*, buying and selling land is the context. Tyler's group uses a sheet of grid chart paper to track their work and show their new maps of the two sections. Tyler, as spokesperson, uses the visual to justify the response to each clue and show what each transaction involved. He uses math terms associated with fractions to announce the number of acres owned by each person and how that amount was determined.

My expectations for talking about mathematics in small groups are clear and doable. Students know that I will be circulating around the room while they are working and that I expect to hear them talking about math. I state explicitly that their math vocabulary should be growing, that I am listening for more and more sophisticated language as we push through the year. I ask them to use this vocabulary in their daily reflections. (If I don't ask them to be aware of how others are using math vocabulary, they won't notice it at all!)

Students understand that when they are working in a group or with a partner, they should address their conversations to each other and ignore my presence unless I ask for their attention. Since I know this is a difficult thing to do at any age, we practice it. I want them to be self-conscious only about how they're using mathematics language. I comment specifically on good examples (either at the time or after I've reviewed my notes) and remind them when I'm not hearing enough. I also offer specific comments, suggestions, and guidelines for the work ahead.

The Whole Class

Whole class discussions also provide opportunities for developing students' math vocabulary. When I am presenting a math challenge or attempting to clarify a concept for the entire class, students are responsible for listening carefully and asking me to define or interpret terms they do not understand.

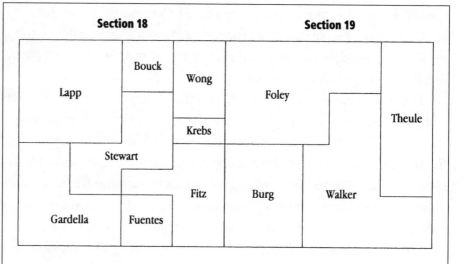

Section 18 **Section 19**

Bouck
Wong
Lapp
Foley
Theule
Krebs
Stewart
Fitz   Burg   Walker
Gardella   Fuentes

Some of the owners of land in sections 18 and 19 sold their land to other people who already owned land in these sections. The clues below describe the results of several transactions.

Clue 1 When all the sales are completed, four people—Theule, Fuentes, Wong, and Gardella—own all of the land in the two sections.

Clue 2 Theule bought from one person and now owns land equivalent to $\frac{1}{2}$ of one section.

Clue 3 Fuentes bought from three people and now owns the equivalent of $\frac{13}{32}$ of one section.

Clue 4 Gardella now owns the equivalent of $\frac{1}{2}$ of a section.

Clue 5 Wong now owns all of the rest of the land in the two sections.

Clue 6 Each of the four owners can walk around all of their land without having to cross onto another person's land.

A. Use the clues to determine what transactions took place. Determine exactly which pieces of land Theule, Fuentes, Wong, and Gardella bought, and explain how you know you are correct.

B. Draw a new map of the two sections, outlining the land belonging to each of the four owners. Tell how many acres each person now owns.

FIGURE 2–5 *Investigation 4 Problem 4.2 Redrawing the Map, From the Bits and Pieces II Unit of the* Connected Mathematics *Series*

I set them up for this early in the year by purposefully including terms they are unlikely to know. *If in doubt, always ask* is the mantra. Of course, they are to do the same when listening to each other.

Listening

While hearing occurs automatically with normally functioning ears, listening to what you're hearing requires a conscious commitment. Listening is enormously important in learning (and in just about any social endeavor). In the classroom, students' relatively short attention spans, combined with peer distractions, confound effective listening. This is especially true during whole-class sharing. Therefore, I pay attention to teaching listening skills.

Sometimes I use the vocabulary version of "I Have, Who Has?" (see Chapter 3) as a class warm-up. The students enjoy being timed and invariably ask to do the exercise again so they can improve their time, and are chagrined when their time does not improve. I seize the moment to talk about better listening skills, asking students for their ideas on what will improve listening. These are representative responses:

- ◆ Think about what you expect to hear.
- ◆ Concentrate.
- ◆ Stop talking.
- ◆ Make eye contact with the speaker.
- ◆ Review before starting.
- ◆ Practice the part you're going to read.
- ◆ Actually listen.

The only one of these ideas that cannot be generalized to most situations is practicing what you will be reading. It is, however, an insightful recognition of the role a speaker plays in the listening process relative to both the pacing and the clarity of what is said. A respectful relationship between listener and speaker enhances both the listening and speaking processes. Good eye contact and attention from the listener supports and encourages a speaker, and effective speaking engages and supports good listening.

I also ask my students about their *distraction demons*: noises, annoying movements, "spacing out." Enough said. Students are quite capable of identifying the issues and reminding themselves of their personal responsibility for eliminating distractions.

Two other strategies I use to increase attention and improve listening skills are *note taking* and *paraphrasing*. Student responsibility for taking notes is outlined in "Expectations for Mathematics" and "Student Guidelines for Mathematics Journals and Binder" (see Chapter 5 for details and examples). Students are routinely held accountable for class notes, and their journals are collected at least once each month. However, I find paraphrasing to be the most concrete and effective tool for improving listening skills. Students enjoy the challenge of accurately restating or summarizing a previous contributor. Paraphrasing is a good opportunity to use the vocabulary and is also a tool for building student self-confidence when it comes to classroom contributions.

Clarifying Expectations

Another effective strategy for maximizing the quality of classroom conversations is to develop a rubric, a simple description of the highest level of performance. Together my students and I work through a four-step process:

1. *Brainstorm*. I ask students to think about the characteristics of a good math conversation (one that would rate a thumbs-up from the principal) for either a small group or the entire class. We chart the characteristics until the possibilities are exhausted.

2. *Prioritize*. We study the list and combine closely related characteristics. Together we decide which of the characteristics is most important, second most important, and so on, up to six. That's enough to keep in mind when preparing for group conversation.

3. *Fine-tune.* As the teacher having final authority and responsibility for the classroom, I refine the list for publication.

4. *Implement.* The list is posted in the classroom as a constant reminder of expectations. (A three-hole-punched copy is also placed in each student's binder.) In addition, every week or so we assess ourselves as a class and state evidence for the presence of each ideal characteristic.

Here are some representative student-brainstormed characteristics:

◆ Energetic.

◆ Everyone contributes.

◆ Sit so you can see everyone—semicircular.

◆ The topic is fun but challenging.

◆ No one is talking amongst themselves.

◆ Everyone speaks so others understand them and know what they're talking about.

◆ A point is proven or disproved—staying on the topic.

◆ Everyone listens and focuses.

◆ Good arguments with evidence.

◆ No fooling around with the hands.

◆ Generally positive and respectful—no one yells.

◆ Accept different ideas.

We refine this list and choose the following six points as most important (if students do not mention mathematics vocabulary during the brainstorm, I bring it up during the prioritizing conversation to make sure it has a prominent position):

◆ Speakers use appropriate mathematics vocabulary and speak so they can be understood.

◆ The topic is challenging and interesting.

◆ Everyone is able to see everyone else.

- Everyone listens, remains focused, and is respectfully attentive.
- Contributors use good arguments with evidence to prove or disprove a point.
- Everyone contributes, and different ideas are accepted.

Former teacher Marlene Thier used similar tools to help students learn science. In her book *The New Science Literacy* (2002), she calls her brief lists *performance expectations.* Although they may not be student-generated, they are used effectively to "focus the attention of students and teachers on key skills of literacy that necessarily are called upon in the course of good science teaching and learning" (28–29). Of particular relevance to our student-generated rubric for quality mathematics conversations is her "Performance Expectations for Group Interaction" (80–81):

- *Take turns,* adopting and relinquishing tasks and roles appropriately.
- *Actively solicit others' comments and opinions.* Successful group work results from the participation and contributions of every member.
- *Offer your own opinions forcefully* but without dominating. There is a difference between being assertive and being overbearing.
- *Respond appropriately* to comments and questions. Be courteous, modulate the give-and-take of discussion, and use the listening skills outlined previously.
- *Volunteer contributions and respond when asked* by the teacher or peers. Group members must contribute constructively.
- *Expand on responses* when asked to do so and give group members similar opportunities.
- *Be able to use evidence and give reasons* in support of opinions expressed.
- *Employ group decision-making techniques,* such as brainstorming or an appropriate problem-solving sequence (such as recognizing a problem, defining it, identifying possible solutions, selecting the optimal solution, implementing the solution, and then evaluating the result).

◆ *Work with other group members to divide labor* in order to achieve overall group goals efficiently.

Whatever format is used to spell out the expected conditions and behavior for good math conversations, the most important thing is to use the resulting rubric. When students understand what is expected, math dialogues improve. Nevertheless, frequent reminders are necessary. It's best to point to the characteristics before each class summary or oral activity when you first begin to use this tool. It's also helpful for students and teacher to assess themselves once a week or every two weeks, pointing out areas of strength and weakness and targeting specific elements for improvement.

. . . .

Chapter 3

What About Deliberate Vocabulary Work?

*Learning the words of mathematics need not be a burden.
Words are a natural part of human activity; they have
histories, relations to one another, and connections to the
real world. Students can appreciate language and value its
role in supporting communication and understanding
when they are engaged in inventing, visualizing, and
studying the history, uses, and connections of words.*

—Rheta N. Rubenstein (1996, 218)

NCTM's *Curriculum and Evaluation Standards for School Mathematics* (1989) tells us that middle-level students need to demonstrate "increasing sophistication in the ability to communicate mathematics." It also states clearly that "this development cannot occur without deliberate and careful acquisition of the language of mathematics" (78). Students encounter the language of mathematics in many places and in many ways: school math problems, family conversations, product advertisements, and so on. Coming to know these words happens over time, and if we fail to pay deliberate attention to them, many of them may fall between the cracks.

As teachers, we continuously track the progress and needs of our students and make our instructional decisions accordingly. Hearing the words of mathematics used in easy, unassuming discourse is an important immersion tactic on its own, and it also reveals gaps in mathematics nomenclature and related conceptual understanding. When such a gap becomes apparent, it's a signal to put more focus on the words—the language that fleshes out the missing conceptual picture. I use a number of mathematics vocabulary lessons that are indeed deliberate about meeting, learning, and coming to know mathematics words. These tactics are the front door to my immersion program. Their sole purpose is to expand my students' mathematics vocabulary. I also make a special effort to help my students master the *demons*—certain mathematics vocabulary terms that are extraordinarily difficult for most students.

Once they have been introduced to a series of new technical terms, students need to practice the words in more than casual ways. Knowing that, I devote a reasonably balanced amount of time to vocabulary practice. Cognitive research has revealed the kind of practice that yields long-term gains. Psychologist Hermann Ebbinghaus first noted the *spacing effect* in 1885 while studying memory. His work led to the concept of *distributed practice* as opposed to *massed practice*. Research over the years has continued to show that brief practice sessions distributed over time result in significantly better memory and recall of material than long concentrated periods of practice (Willingham 2002). Several strategies in this chapter purposefully spread vocabulary practice over many class periods.

Collaborative Minilessons on the Four Operations

Diagnosing and remedying are two of the best parts of teaching. The challenge of responding to a specific need is energizing. Assessing possible resources, designing a program, and introducing an unexpected element to the classroom creates tension, gets the students' attention, and recharges everyone's batteries.

Mid-September of a recent school year I noticed a significant discrepancy between my expectation of what students should know about the four operations with whole numbers and the understanding evidenced in their work and in our class conversations. Gentle probing uncovered an even more remarkable range of basic operation sense and knowledge. It was a dramatic decision-making moment. I did not want to take time out from the seventh- and eighth-grade curriculum to address the language and related conceptual understanding of whole-number operations. But I needed a compromise strategy; otherwise this gap could be a barrier to our study of rational numbers. Time constraints, the constant need to expand my students' mathematics vocabulary, and the desire to work from a base of student knowledge led me to create a series of five- to ten-minute minilessons to be conducted at the beginning of each class.

First, I made an informal outline of the four operations on whole numbers and the relationships among them on five-by-eight-inch index cards (see Figure 3–1). I instructed the students to begin a section in their journal—The Four Binary Operations and the Relationships Among Them—that they would add to daily until we had completed the minilesson series.

Then using the cards as my guide, I asked students to think about when they first began adding. What did they know about addition? How did they think it related to real life? What language did they use to talk about addition? What did they call the various elements of an addition computation? How might a mathematician generalize the process of addition? As students responded to these questions I recorded their ideas on chart paper. I asked for real-life examples, and we translated them to number sentences. I asked them what would happen if we changed the position of the addends. We physically modeled it in class with small groups of students as a way to introduce the idea of properties. Once the initial minilesson was finished, students immediately wanted to know if they could include some of the words we had used in their vocabulary lists. I was thrilled, and encouraged them to do so: I was sure the strategy was going to work!

We completed each minilesson of the series with whole numbers before we went on to companion lessons dealing with rational numbers. For example, we established the inverse relationship for the addition and subtraction of whole numbers before we tackled student-designed algorithms for the addition and subtraction of fractions, decimals, and percents. As a result, the students widened their understanding and gained an amazing new confidence. They enjoyed attaching more sophisticated language to work they had been doing for years and looked at all computation through new eyes. Their mental math skills showed dramatic improvement as well.

The greatest bonus was the confidence with which they approached the division of fractions before any formal instruction. Their favorite vocabulary term was *multiplicative inverse,* because of the way it sounded—they simply loved saying it and looked for every opportunity to use it.

At the end of the trimester, when preparing their portfolios, most of the students chose to include notes from the minilessons (see the example in Figure 3–2) as evidence of their growing note-taking skills.

This series of minilessons was an exhilarating teaching experience because the students were 100 percent engaged in the development of the mathematics. They accumulated an amazing vocabulary record that was used extensively and with confidence from that point on. When we went on to study the four operations with integers later in the year, the work went quickly and surely because of the powerful connections they were able to make.

"I Have, Who Has?"—An Old Friend in a New Hat

Another opportunity to add word knowledge to student repertoires came about when I encountered a version of the classroom game "I Have, Who Has?" that had been adapted to focus on mathematics vocabulary (*Association of Teachers of Mathematics in Maine Newsletter,* Winter 2000). The game requires making a set of cards (see Figure 3–3). The top of each card contains one mathematics term preceded by the words "I have." The bottom of each card lists a definition—unrelated to the term at the top of the card—in the form of a question, after the words "Who has."

The game (exercise, really) goes like this: The cards are randomly distributed among students. Everyone gets at least one card, but many students will have more than one. A student is selected at random to go first. She selects one of her cards (there may only be one), ignores the "I have" at the top, and carefully reads the "Who has" definition. Students must focus and listen carefully to decide whether the definition matches one of their words. The person who has the word being defined calls out "I have" followed by the word. That person then reads the "Who has" definition on her card. The game continues until all the definitions have been read. The cards are

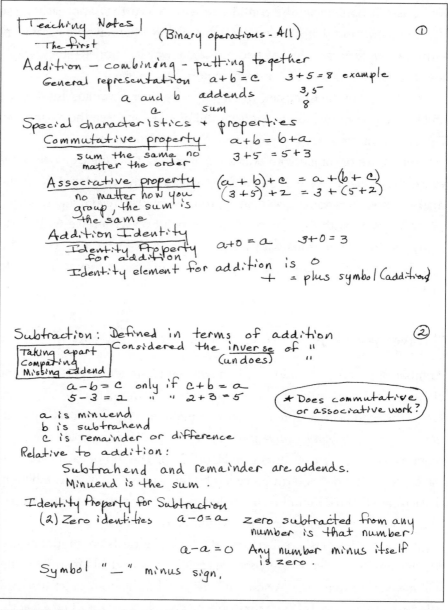

Teaching Notes
~~The first~~   (Binary operations - All)   ①

Addition — combining - putting together
  General representation $a + b = c$ $3 + 5 = 8$ example
           a and b   addends $\begin{array}{c} 3, 5 \\ \hline 8 \end{array}$
              c   sum
Special characteristics + properties
  Commutative property $a + b = b + a$
     sum the same no $3 + 5 = 5 + 3$
     matter the order
  Associative property $(a + b) + c = a + (b + c)$
     no matter how you $(3 + 5) + 2 = 3 + (5 + 2)$
     group, the sum is
     the same
  Addition Identity
     Identity Property $a + 0 = a$ $3 + 0 = 3$
       for addition
     Identity element for addition is 0
                           + = plus symbol (addition)

Subtraction: Defined in terms of addition   ②
     Considered the inverse of "
  ┌─────────────────┐   (undoes)   "
  │ Taking apart   │
  │ Comparing   │
  │ Missing addend │
  └─────────────────┘
        $a - b = c$ only if $c + b = a$ ⎛ ＊ Does commutative ⎞
        $5 - 3 = 2$ "   " $2 + 3 = 5$ ⎝ or associative work? ⎠
     a is minuend
     b is subtrahend
     c is remainder or difference
Relative to addition:
        Subtrahend and remainder are addends.
        Minuend is the sum.

Identity Property for Subtraction
   (2) Zero identities $a - 0 = a$ zero subtracted from any
                                        number is that number
                          $a - a = 0$ Any number minus itself
                                        is zero.
   Symbol " — " minus sign.

FIGURE 3–1   *Informal Outline Used to Guide Collaborative Minilessons on the Four Operations and the Relationships Among Them*

Multiplication :　　　　　　　(3)

| repeated addition |
| equal sets (groups) |
| rectangular arrays |
| equal linear moves |

$a \times b = c$ 　　　　　$3 \times 5 = 15$
　　a, b factors　　　　$3, 5$ factors
　　　c product　　　　15 product
　　　　(multiple)　　　(multiple of $3 + 5$)

a multiplier (# of groups)
b multiplicand (size of group)
c product (multiple)

Special properties:
　　Commutative
　　Associative
　　Zero property　$a \times 0 = 0$
　　Identity property for mult. $a \times 1 = a$
　　Identity element for multiplication　1
　　Reciprocal or multiplicative inverse:
　　　　Any two numbers whose product is 1
　　　　$2 \times \frac{1}{2} = 1$　$\frac{1}{2}$ is the reciprocal of 2.
　　Distributive Property combines mult and add or
　　　　　　　　　　　　　　　mult and sub.

　　　Use tile example: Rectangle $3 \times 5 = 3 \times (1 + 4)$
　　　　　　Separate 5 into 1+4　　　$= (3 \times 1) + (3 \times 4)$

Division : Defined only in terms of multiplication　　(4)

| Separates/ |
| Takes apart |

$a \div b = c$ only if $c \times b = a$
　　　　　　(iff)
Inverse of multiplication or repeated subtraction
　　$12 \div 3 = 4$　because $4 \times 3 = 12$

　　a is dividend　product
　　b is divisor　　factor
　　c is quotient　factor

　　Written 3 ways:　$\frac{a}{b} = c$　$b\overline{)a}^{c}$　$a \div b = c$

Find - Size of group　or　number of groups
　　　　partition　　　　　measurement

　　Identities　$a \div a = 1$　$a \div 1 = a$　$0 \div a = 0$

　　Division by $\emptyset$ not defined
　　　　　　zero　$a \div 0 = ? \rightarrow$ can't get back
　　　　　　　　　　　　　　　　　to 'a'

FIGURE 3–1　*continued.*

CONTINUED...

The 4 operations and the   104
relationships between them

<u>SUBTRACTION</u>   the minus
                                                sign
- taking apart or away
- comparing
- find missing addend
<u>Inverse of addition</u>
    $a - b = c$ only if $c + b = a$
    $5 - 3 = 2$ only if $2 + 3 = 5$
• $b, c =$ addens $-b$, subtrahend {c, remander (taking away)
• $a =$ sum $-a$, minuend { difference (comparing)
<u>properties</u>   10-6
    Identity $a - 0 = a$
              $a - a = 0$
    element $= 0$

<u>MULTIPLICATION</u>   10-13
repeated addition: * Rectangular arrays
example → • $9 + 9 + 9 + 9 = 4 \times 9$ 2 [grid] 2×4 or 4×2
                                      x 4
equal sets: *The area model
(circles) 4×3 •The linear model $\frac{4 \quad 4 \quad 4}{3 \times 4 = 12}$
$a \times b = c$ a- multiplier } a and b are
$3 \times 5 = 15$ b- multiplicand } factors
                     c- product
a (# of group) $c =$ multiple of a, b
b (#size of group)

FIGURE 3–2   *Audrey's Journal Notes From Collaborative Minilessons on Multiplication and Division*

continued

Multpication   10·18

Special Properties

Commutative property

$a \times b = b \times a$ (order

$2 \times 3 = 3 \times 2$

Associative Property

$(a \times b) \times c = a \times (b \times c)$

$(3 \times 2) \times 4 = 3 \times (2 \times 4)$

$6 \times 4 = 3 \times 8$

(element) Identity properties

$e = 1$

multiplication Identity $a \times 1 = a$ or $1 \times a = a$

$14 \times 1 = 14$ or $1 \times 14 = 14$

zero Identity $0 \times a = 0$ or $a \times 0 = 0$

$0 \times 9 = 0$ or $9 \times 0 = 0$

• Reciprocal or Multiplicative Inverse

examples $a \times \frac{1}{a} = 1$ $2 \times \frac{1}{2} = 1$

↳ $47 \times \frac{1}{47} = 1$

- Distributive Property

combines multiplication and addition or

Subtraction

$a \times (b+c)$

$a(b+c) = a(b) + a(c)$

$a(3+1) = 2(3) + 2(1)$

$2(4) = 6 + 2$

$2(2+2) = 2(2) + 2(2)$

$2(4) = 4 + 4$

FIGURE 3–2   *continued.*

continued

10.20

Symbols for multiplying

× with whole numbers

• variables and where "x" might be confusing

( ) $a(b+2)$ $2(3+1)$ $2(3)$

. ab 2 or more variables

✱ technology

Division

separates, takes appart

Defined only in terms of multiplication

$a \div b = c$ only if $c \times b = a$

$12 \div 3 = 4$ only if $4 \times 3 = 12$

Division by 0 is not defined or possible
(zero)

Inverse of multiplication

Repeated subtraction   - Measurment division

a = dividend } Product   (Repeated subtraction)

b = divisor)   - Partition division
             } factor
c = quotient)   (taking fractional parts)

$a \div b = c$

$a/b = c$

$b\overline{)a}^{c}$ properties:

$0 \div a = 0$ if $0 \times a = 0$

• Identities $a - 1 = a, a \div a = 1$

• distribute protery $(a+b) \div c = (a \div c) + (b \div c)$

$(6+4) \div 2 = (6 \div 2) + (4 \div 2)$

FIGURE 3–2 _continued._

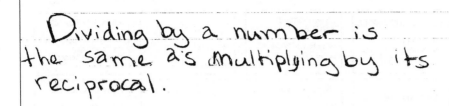

Dividing by a number is the same as multiplying by its reciprocal.

FIGURE 3–2 *continued.*

designed so that the student who began the game will have the final word at the top of the beginning card.

My students loved the game and put their own stamp on it by striving to reduce the amount of time it took the class to complete a round. It was the best kind of peer pressure, because they found encouraging ways to support (*coach*) each other. They practiced reading their definitions so they could be heard clearly; they practiced pronouncing the terms correctly; and they helped those who were insecure with certain word meanings.

After the success of this game, it seemed only natural to create a vocabulary game of our own using terms we were in the process of learning. So, working from a brainstormed list of vocabulary, everyone selected a different word. The students' homework assignment was to write a definition that would distinguish their term from all the other selected terms. Collectively pondering the task, we set the following criteria: Write the definition so that classmates will understand it; check dictionaries for accuracy of meaning; and keep the definition as concise as possible. At this point the term *elegant* came together with the ideas of *necessary and sufficient*—saying enough but not too much.

The process of preparing the game included peer critiques of the definitions and subsequent revisions. I verified and fine-tuned the definitions before they were recorded on the lower, "Who has," portion of three-by-five-inch cards. Then I randomly assigned words, written in pencil, to the top, "I have," portion of the cards (see Figure 3–4). The cards were then distributed, tested, and adjusted as necessary. Testing is critical in order to make certain the game will encompass all of the cards. Once the class

I have RIGHT ANGLE. Who has the lines which intersect to form 90 degree angles?	**I have OBTUSE ANGLE.** Who has an 8-sided polygon?	**I have $\frac{22}{7}$.** Who has lines in a plane that never intersect?	**I have TRAPEZOID.** Who has a chord of a circle which goes through the center?
I have PERPENDICULAR LINES. Who has a five-sided polygon?	**I have OCTAGON.** Who has the instrument used to construct circles?	**I have PARALLEL LINES.** Who has an angle with exactly 180 degrees?	**I have DIAMETER.** Who has two figures which have the same shape but different sizes?
I have PENTAGON. Who has the point where two rays meet to form an angle?	**I have COMPASS.** Who has the type of triangle with all angles less than 90 degrees?	**I have STRAIGHT ANGLE.** Who has two angles whose measures have a sum of 180 degrees?	**I have SIMILAR FIGURES.** Who has a triangle with all sides of different lengths?
I have VERTEX. Who has the value of pi to hundredths place?	**I have ACUTE TRIANGLE.** Who has the sum of the measures of the interior angles of a triangle?	**I have SUPPLEMENTARY ANGLES.** Who has a triangle with two sides congruent?	**I have SCALENE TRIANGLE.** Who has two angles whose measures have a sum of 90 degrees?
I have 3.14. Who has the point which separates a line segment into two congruent segments?	**I have 180 degrees.** Who has a rectangle with 4 congruent sides?	**I have ISOSCELES TRIANGLE.** Who has a 10-sided polygon?	**I have COMPLEMENTARY ANGLES.** Who has a 9-sided polygon?
I have MIDPOINT. Who has a flat surface which continues infinitely in all directions?	**I have SQUARE.** Who has a line segment from the center of a circle to a point on the circle?	**I have DECAGON.** Who has a parallelogram with all sides congruent?	**I have NONAGON.** Who has a quadrilateral with opposite sides parallel and congruent?
I have PLANE. Who has the instrument used to measure an angle in degrees?	**I have RADIUS.** Who has a polygon with 6 sides?	**I have RHOMBUS.** Who has a line segment (other than a side) which joins two vertices of a polygon?	**I have PARALLELOGRAM.** Who has figures with exactly the same shape and same size?
I have PROTRACTOR. Who has the type of angle with more than 90 degrees but less than 180 degrees?	**I have HEXAGON.** Who has pi as a fraction?	**I have DIAGONAL.** Who has a quadrilateral with only two parallel sides?	**I have CONGRUENT FIGURES.** Who has an angle of exactly 90 degrees?

FIGURE 3–3   *"I Have, Who Has?" Vocabulary Exercise*

learned how to complete a set of thirty or so terms and definitions, I gave interested students extra credit for creating sets in other strands.

This activity is a great match with *spaced* practice. We frequently use "I Have, Who Has?" as a class warm-up. It takes no more than five minutes to complete a round, and the benefits are many. The students prepare for the game by helping each other review word meanings, and they learn terms they are then able to use during class discussions. For example, when talking about characteristics of circles recently, Molly reminded the class that "a diameter is also a chord, the special one that goes through the center."

Concept Maps

Twice a year, at the end of the first two trimesters, I hold portfolio conferences with students and their caregivers. The portfolios are prepared during the final week of the trimester. It is an intensive time for revisiting the major work completed during the period. I specify one or two required entries, but all the rest are up to the individual students, and they know they will be asked to explain their choices.

While preparing for one of these portfolio conferences, I realized that the students needed a new tool for organizing and sharing what they now understood about the four operations and their relationships. We brainstormed all of the terms we had revisited or met for the first time during our collaborative minilessons and listed them on chart paper. Then I went to the whiteboard and wrote the word *operations* in the center. I introduced the strategy of concept mapping and asked the students for ideas to use as a starting point.

I made it clear that our concept maps were to be simple. We wouldn't annotate them but would use the visual relationships that emerged as a guide to remembering what we had learned. After we worked through an example on the whiteboard, I sent them off to create (as homework) their own concept maps based on the suggestions of classmates, their own experiences, or their own creative ideas. Whatever information they included (and there were many possibilities), the visual display had to show the four operational relationships. Once each student and I had discussed and edited the personal concept map, it went into the portfolio, to be used by the student as a visual aid to explain what he or she had learned to the parents or caregivers attending the conference. Two examples of student concept maps on the four basic operations are included in Figure 3–5.

TERM	DEFINITION
Base ten	I have RAY Who has—a number system using 10 symbols, 0 through 9, where each place has a value that is a power of 10?
Circumscribe	I have COEFFICIENT Who has—drawing a line around a figure while touching but not cutting into it?
Coefficient	I have PRIME FACTORIZATION Who has—a number that is multiplied by a variable in an equation or expression?
Composite	I have IRRATIONAL NUMBER Who has—a number with more than two factors?
Congruent	I have INEQUALITIES Who has—two figures that are the same size and shape?
Convex polygon	I have EQUIANGULAR Who has—a polygon with all edges going outwards rather than inwards?
Dividend	I have VERTEX Who has—the number being divided?
Equiangular	I have INSCRIBED Who has—a closed figure whose angles all have the same measure?
Exterior angle of a polygon	I have COMPOSITE Who has—the angle formed when a side of a polygon is extended beyond the vertex to make another angle with the adjacent side?
Inequalities	I have DIVIDEND Who has—mathematical expressions that include greater than or less than symbols?
Inscribed	I have TERMINATING Who has—an angle or polygon whose vertices are part of another figure?
Irrational number	I have TRANSFORMATIONS Who has—a real number that cannot be named as the ratio of two integers such as Pi or the square root of two?
Octahedron	I have CONVEX POLYGON Who has—a polyhedron with eight faces?

FIGURE 3–4 *Study Sheets for a Class-Generated Version of "I Have, Who Has?" Using Vocabulary Chosen by Students*

TERM	DEFINITION
Palindrome	I have VOLUME Who has—a number that reads the same forwards or backwards?
Planar	I have CIRCUMSCRIBE Who has—a term that relates to a flat surface like a table top that is imagined as stretching forever?
Prime factorization	I have CONGRUENT Who has—the prime factors that if you multiply together equal the number?
Pythagorean triple	I have STEM-AND-LEAF PLOT Who has—sets of numbers that satisfy the Pythagorean Theorem, $a^2 + b^2 = c^2$?
Ray	I have PLANAR Who has—a part of a line that has one endpoint and extends infinitely in one direction?
Relatively prime	I have BASE TEN Who has—numbers that share only one as a common factor?
Scientific notation	I have PALINDROME Who has—a number written as the product of a number greater than or equal to one but less than ten, and a power of ten?
Stem-and-leaf plot	I have SUPPLEMENTARY ANGLES Who has—a base-ten system for collecting and organizing data that has a wide range?
Supplementary angles	I have SCIENTIFIC NOTATION Who has—two angles that have a sum of 180 degrees?
Terminating decimal	I have EXTERIOR ANGLE OF A POLYGON Who has—a decimal number with a finite number of digits?
Transformations	I have PYTHAGOREAN TRIPLE Who has—a change from one expression or function to another while maintaining equality or similar configuration?
Vertex	I have OCTAHEDRON Who has—the point where two line segments, lines, or rays meet?
Volume	I have RELATIVELY PRIME Who has—the amount of space or capacity of a three-dimensional figure measured in cubic units?

FIGURE 3–4 *continued.*

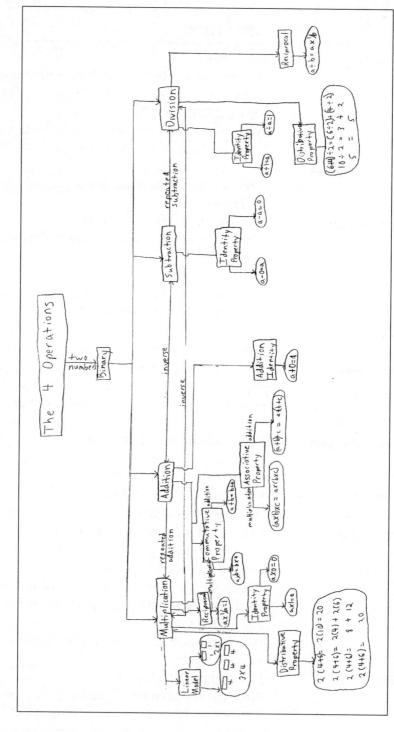

FIGURE 3-5 *Portfolio Concept Maps on the Four Operations by Tyler and Zephyr Illustrating Individual Interpretation, Level of Detail, and Organization*

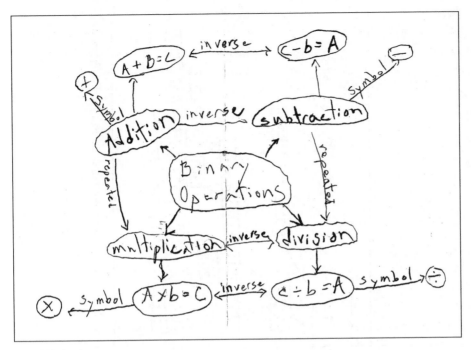

FIGURE 3–5   *continued.*

Next, I divided the class into groups of three so that the students could practice their presentations, each student in turn making an oral presentation while the remaining two played the roles of parents. One group volunteered to model the process in front of the class. The role-playing parents got into their parts and asked typical probing questions. It was much more interesting than anyone expected. We could not have found a better way to practice using the language of mathematics in a meaningful way. During the actual conferences, students made confident presentations and parents expressed appreciation for having learned about mathematical relationships they had previously never really understood.

The following trimester we studied *similarity* in depth and once again had a significant collection of mathematical terms related to this focus. The students suggested that it would be great if they could prepare concept maps for their portfolio presentations. (Two examples are included in Figure 3–6.) In this instance, the maps helped students distinguish between *scale*

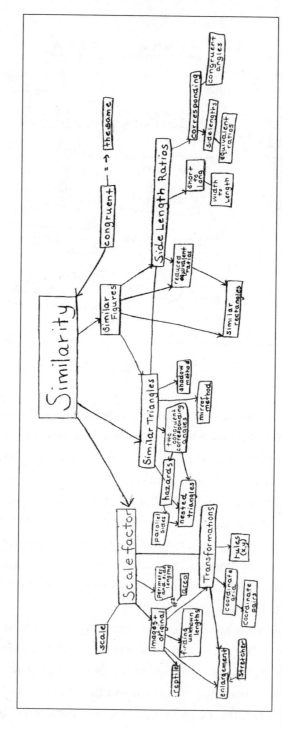

FIGURE 3–6 *Portfolio Concept Maps on Similarity by Brenna and Nick Showing Their Personal Choices for Emphasis and Organization*

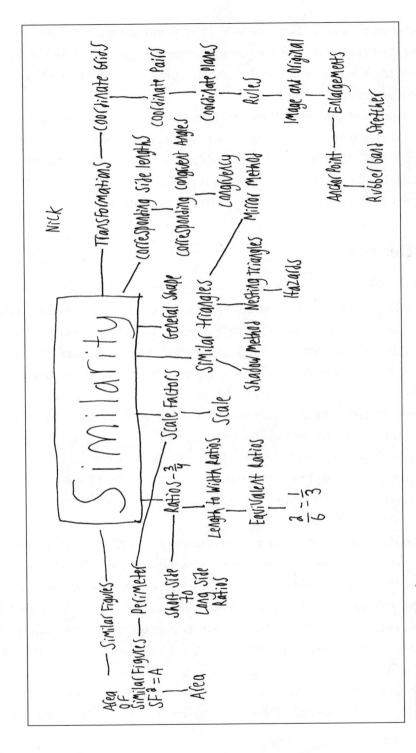

FIGURE 3–6 *continued.*

and *scale factor* and go on to deliver credible and impressive explanations during their conferences. (One parent commented that his child was performing mathematical thinking the parent hadn't encountered until he was in graduate school!)

Creating concept maps gives students several focused opportunities to construct their own mathematical understanding—the vocabulary words are the bricks while the conceptual relationships and connections are the mortar. In addition, the vocabulary practice is repeated over time: brainstorming, mapping, revising, practicing, role-playing, and conferencing.

The Demons

Certain math demons—terms that are confusing, misinterpreted, or incorrectly interchanged—require extraordinary attention. Teachers are constantly being challenged to find ways to make sure that students understand these difficult terms, and there are many wonderful articles in education magazines on specific strategies teachers have tried in their classrooms. Two pairs of demon terms my students invariably have trouble with are *area/perimeter* and *factor/multiple.* There are others as well, but in my years of teaching these are the ones that have caused the most concern.

In the case of *area* and *perimeter*, I have developed a companion art lesson involving lines and two-dimensional shapes. The big idea is to make a tactile connection between *perimeter* and something that is *linear* and between *area* and a filled-in *region.*

We start with an etymological introduction to *linear,* tracing the word's history to *flax, linum* in Latin, or to Roman *linen thread, linea.* "Left to its own devices, thread is likely to twist or curl, and so the word *line* could mean what we now call a *curve.* When pulled taut, however, thread can be made to approximate a true (= straight) line." Furthermore, "the derived adjective *linear* means having to do with or being in the shape of a line" (Schwartzman 1994, 127).

Because I have a ready source for flax (the Old Sturbridge Village, Sturbridge, Massachusetts), I give each student a piece. We bend the straw to remove the fibers and twist them to understand how they are spun into linen thread. We then cut a ball of ordinary string into eighteen-inch lengths, which we rub thoroughly with a piece of colorful soft chalk. Finally we prepare variously shaped oaktag stencils representing planar regions.

The students then create designs out of lines and shapes using two techniques: They stretch the chalked string tightly over a plain sheet of paper and snap it to produce chalk lines, and they place one or more of the stencils on the paper, rub a small amount of chalk in the center of each, and spread the chalk to the edges of the stencil with a tissue. (See Figure 3–7.) The resulting designs are mostly abstract, but some are more realistic. We

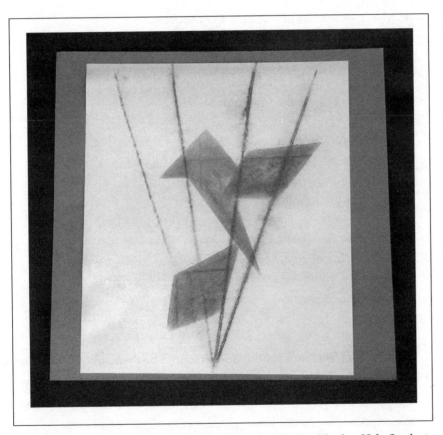

FIGURE 3–7 *Example of a Regional and Linear Design Used to Help Students Distinguish Between Characteristics of Figures with Measures of Area and Those with Measures of Perimeter or Length.* Set Photo by Donald Murray.

Student Ideas About Factors and Multiples

◆ Multiples are bigger than the number. Factors are smaller. [Always?]

◆ Factors are what you multiply to get a number.

◆ Factors only go up as high as the number. Multiples go past the number.

◆ Multiples are all the numbers that you get when you multiply the number by other whole numbers to get a product.

◆ Factors are all the whole numbers that you multiply together to equal that number.

◆ Factors are the whole numbers that make up a number by using multiplication.

◆ Multiples are the products of the number.

◆ Factors are the whole numbers you multiply to get the number.

◆ Factors are divisors of the number.

◆ Multiples are higher than the number. [All?]

◆ Factors are lower than the number [all?] and can go into the number evenly.

◆ Factors are what you can multiply to get the number.

◆ Multiples are any number(s) that is (are) divisible by a certain number.

◆ Multiples are infinite. Factors are not.

◆ Factors are the opposite of multiples. [In what ways?]

FIGURE 3–8 *A list of student-generated ideas for distinguishing factors from multiples. Brackets indicate the need for reflection and discussion.*

then discuss which elements of the design would be measured in linear units and which would be measured in regional units. As we develop various strategies and formulas relative to perimeter and area, the designs are a handy, attractive reference for distinguishing between perimeter and area, linear and regional, and one-dimensional and two-dimensional properties.

For the factor/multiple demon, my number one strategy, once number theory has been studied or reviewed, is regular (at least twice a week) factor/

multiple warm-ups: listing factors and the first ten multiples for an interesting pair of numbers; determining their greatest common factor; and determining their least common multiple. As part of this brief but meaningful practice session, we talk about how factors for any number are *fewer and finite*, while multiples are *many and infinite*—more great mathematical language, with some alliteration thrown in!

One year I had the students write their favorite ideas for distinguishing between factors and multiples on three-by-five-inch cards. I collected the cards, typed up the ideas (many of their statements were similar, but I carefully recorded each one in order to recognize their contributions), and distributed the list to everyone. Every year since, this list (see Figure 3–8) has been part of the forms and guides section of the student binders. The bracketed queries are excellent discussion prompts.

Students encounter mathematics language in a variety of venues. They experience the majority during formal mathematics class activities but some terms come from random events such as the MATHCOUNTS program, the menu of problems in the middle school math journal, a family conversation, and so on. Moving from a specific focus on word study to a diverse assortment of writing opportunities allows and encourages students to incorporate the terms into their regular mathematical communications.

Pushing the Vocabulary:
Going for Breadth and Depth Through Writing

*[Bring words] back alive in their native habitat, the
wilderness of written expression in which they roam.*
— MAXWELL NURNBERG (1998, 4)

CHAPTER 4

Problem-Solving Write-Ups

It is important to give students experiences that help them appreciate the power and precision of mathematical language. . . . Language is as important to learning mathematics as it is to learning to read.

—NATIONAL COUNCIL OF TEACHERS OF MATHEMATICS
(2000, 63, 128)

Writing is a powerful tool for unleashing the mathematician within each student. I've seen it happen surprisingly fast (as with Anne, whom you'll read about later), but usually it happens over time and requires persistence from a "nagging" teacher. It helps to establish a pattern early on whereby students know they are to document their thinking with mathematical language. When this becomes the norm, students think more deeply about the mathematics they're doing and how they make sense of it. Writing becomes a major venue for the meaningful use of technical math terminology. The writing rituals are a framework for tracking the development and use of mathematics vocabulary. At the same time, writing is a platform for showing how vocabulary growth is entwined with the growth of conceptual understanding.

Why Write

Recent mathematics curriculums, grounded in the most current research on teaching and learning, require mathematics writing competency, which in turn calls for an ever expanding vocabulary. For example, the following prompt is found at the conclusion of every investigation in every unit of the grades 6 through 8 *Connected Mathematics* program: "Think about your answers to these questions, discuss your ideas with other students and your teacher, and then *write a summary* of your findings in your journal." In addition, most problems and homework assignments within each investigation end with "Explain your answer [or how you got your answer]," "Explain your reasoning," or "Describe the method you used and why you think your method works."

"The Language of Numbers," a unit from *Seeing and Thinking Mathematically in the Middle Grades*, reveals similar expectations: "Do you think the mystery device number system uses place value? Explain why or why not" (42); "Pick one mystery number puzzle you solved. Find all the possible answers. Explain how you know that you found all the possible answers" (35).

Newer state assessments reflect this requirement as well. California was the forerunner of this type of assessment. Figure 4–1a is an item from the 1987 California Assessment Program, along with a description of the general expectations for student responses. It is clear that students need to be comfortable with technical vocabulary to produce an acceptable response. Finally, in a sample item from the Massachusetts Comprehensive Assessment System (MCAS) 2000 test, students are asked twice in a two-part prompt to "explain your reasoning in detail" (Figure 4-1b).

Clearly, students need writing skills and a good mathematics vocabulary to provide responses to these types of questions, responses that will not be acceptable if they appear without appropriate justification and supporting evidence. The days of naked, magical numbers are gone—students can no longer, like Peppermint Patty of the *Peanuts* cartoon, toss wild digits in rapid succession while praying for a mystifying "hit." Writing know-how and facility are also needed to explain one's thinking and solution processes.

Problem A

Imagine you are talking to a student in your class on the telephone and want the student to draw some figures. The other student cannot see the figures. Write a set of directions so that the other student can draw the figures exactly as shown below.

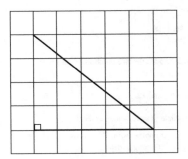 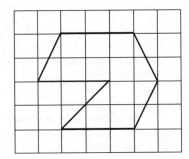

General Expectations

Ability to communicate mathematical ideas with clarity is an important component of mathematical power as emphasized in the California *Mathematics Framework*. Good communication, both verbal and written, indicates understanding. Understanding of a problem and ability to think are prerequisites to successful problem solving.

Problem A assessed the skills of communicating about geometric shapes. It requires students to use effective terminology to describe the necessary features, in correct steps, to reproduce the given geometric shapes. Responses revealed how well students formulated and communicated mathematical ideas. No single solution or method was correct. An effective solution would result in the precise reproduction of the figures. The use of the word *exact* in the problem implied that the student's written directions would preserve the scale and orientation of the figures. It was also hoped that the instructions would be concise, mathematically elegant, and easy to follow.

FIGURE 4–1a   *Item From the 1987 California Assessment Program with a Description of the Desired Elements for an Effective Response*

Mathematics, Grade 8

Session 1, Open-Response Question

8. John is playing a board game that uses a pair of number cubes with sides numbered 1 to 6.

To find how many spaces he can move on the board, he adds the two numbers he rolls. The possible sums are

2, 3, 4, 5, 6, 7, 8, 9, 10, 11, and 12.

a. Are all the sums John can roll equally likely? Explain your reasoning in detail.

b. John needs to roll a sum of exactly 11 in order to get another turn. What is the probability that he will roll a sum of exactly 11? Explain your reasoning in detail.

*Reporting Category/Substrand for Item 8: **Statistics and Probability/Probability (p. 145)***

FIGURE 4–1b   *Open-Response Question From the Massachusetts Comprehensive Assessment System, Spring 2000, Illustrating the Expectation for a Written Mathematical Explanation*

Having students write about the mathematics they are doing produces the following benefits:

- ◆ Thoughtfulness and increased reasoning skills.
- ◆ Active involvement in thinking, making sense, constructing, and learning mathematics.
- ◆ Questions raised and new ideas explored.
- ◆ Use of higher-order thinking while interpreting and explaining data.
- ◆ Clarification, reinforcement, and deepened conceptual understanding.
- ◆ Teacher insights:
      student thinking revealed
      understanding verified or misconceptions uncovered

> student attitudes and needs identified
>
> communication between teacher and individual student

◆ Self-reflection and self-directed learning:

> awareness of what they know, do not know, and need to know
>
> awareness of what they can do, cannot do, and need to learn how to do

◆ Recognition that mathematics has a playful human dimension.

In turn, each of these benefits helps tease out a more abundant and useful mathematics vocabulary.

These benefits mirror conclusions drawn from the work of Ann Enyart, Laura Van Zoest, Marilyn Burns, Joan Countryman, and Peggy House. The efforts of these math educators have been chronicled in numerous publications of the National Council of Teachers of Mathematics (NCTM) and are a prolific source of well-grounded and documented classroom writing opportunities. Their work honors the best and most significant research on teaching and learning in general and mathematics more specifically.

So, how can we help our students understand the value added by using writing as a learning tool and realize that an ever expanding vocabulary is necessary to accomplish this writing? What can we do to make mathematical writing doable for them? Because we can reasonably expect that our students won't have much experience with this kind of writing, we need to use the first days and weeks of school to build a support system.

I give considerable thought to the type of writing to put in place—writing that will induce the use of mathematical language naturally, that will add value to the mathematics and be unified with it. One thing I know for sure, a major part of the writing will be about solving problems.

Problem-Solving Write-Ups

As I mentioned in Chapter 1, during the first week of school I introduce students to the "problem-solving write-up." Summarizing how one solved an interesting problem and shared the solution with one's peers is an important aspect of writing in math class. I often start with the Maximum and

Minimum Products Problem. I pass around an envelope containing nine cards, each bearing a different digit from one to nine. I ask five students to pick one card from the envelope. I record the digits from the chosen cards on the whiteboard, and the students record them in their journals. I then ask the students, for homework, to arrange the digits into a two-digit-by-three-digit multiplication problem that will produce the largest possible product. Once they think they have identified the two factors that meet the criteria, they need to be able to convince me (or anyone else) that their solution is correct. To that end, they need to record in their journals every thought they have about solving the problem and everything they actually do to solve the problem. They enter the challenge in their homework log, and we're off and running!

At the beginning of the next day's class, I ask students to restate the problem as they understand it. After several students share their attempts, I ask everyone to write a statement of the problem in their own words in their journals. The criterion: Anyone who reads their statement, particularly a person who has never heard the problem before, will understand the problem and what it is asking. Students then share their written statements with their table partners, and I ask for volunteers to read their statements aloud.

Next, students share their solutions, and I ask them to explain how they came to their conclusions. I check in with students in several groups. I listen for their use of math terminology and repeat effectively used expressions. I want to know first thoughts, first steps, and what they were learning along the way. I also want to know if any conversations with others helped them to their final solution, if indeed they have one.

Once we've listened to all the ideas so far, I give them the rest of the problem and an extension:

- How can the digits be arranged in order to achieve the smallest product?
- Can a solution be generalized for any five digits that might be drawn? If so, how?
- How many different multiplication products can be generated using the five digits?

Next, I formally introduce the format for a "mathematics write-up" and we talk about these four steps:

1. Restate the problem in your own words.
2. Describe the process or processes you used to solve the problem.
3. Present the solution(s) and accompanying arguments.
4. Generalize, if you can, and suggest extensions.

Since we've already completed the first step together, we begin by talking about describing their problem-solving efforts. I remind them that they were asked to record that information as part of their homework, and tell them I'm eager to hear what they've written. As students share their notes, I point out that they can use this information to complete step 2 of their write-ups and that they must describe what they have attempted even if they are unable to find a solution to the problem.

Then, in step 3, they present their solution or solutions, along with all of the supportive evidence. We call the evidence *arguments* and talk about what that means in relation to their solution so far. In this instance, they need to show the essential multiplication examples (with products) they had to complete to verify the greatest possible product and the least possible product. They also need to explain why the examples they use support their conclusion, using place value terminology in their discussion.

In the final portion of the write-up they are to generalize their solution, if possible. In this case, I have specifically chosen a problem that can be generalized, so that I can model the process. I've also modeled an extension by adding the last part of the problem. Generally, however, when students give a suggestion for an extension in a write-up, they don't need to solve it.

This is a good time to stop and list the mathematics vocabulary words we've heard as we've discussed the problem. This way, students have a handy list of mathematics terminology as they complete their first write-ups. Depending on the difficulty of the problem, I generally give students several days to do this. The problem is almost always a homework assignment stretched over a week's time, with interim opportunities in class to check in with peers and ask me questions. If students are having difficulty with a particular element, such as stating the problem in their own words, I have them work it out in their small groups or with their partners.

Using a Rubric

The first year I used the problem-solving write-up, my students and I developed a general rubric based on our experience with a specific scoring rubric from *It's All Write* (Fendel et al. 1998). I also incorporated suggestions from Stenmark's *Assessment Alternatives in Mathematics* (1989, 19) and Stenmark's *Mathematics Assessment* (1991, 24). I've used this rubric (see Figure 4–2) ever since. Its primary purpose is to guide the writing process, not score results, and again, it resides in the forms and guides section of the students' math binders as a ready reference.

The *exemplary* rating, earning the most points (six), lists the criteria for the ideal written product and serves as a checklist. The "clear, elegant explanation" phrase in the first descriptor inevitably prompts a lively class discussion about the term *elegant,* in which we bring out the special meaning it has associated with mathematics and talk about how this concept of elegance will direct the mathematics writing adventures ahead of us.

Students offer a variety of interpretations based on their prior knowledge, and we consult dictionaries as well. The relevant definitions describe *elegant* as marked by *concision, incisiveness,* and *ingenuity* and meaning "cleverly apt and simple." But what does *concision* mean? Ah, its root is *concise.* This helps us establish the expectation for being brief and to the point, short and clear. However, we also agree that we will need to say quite a bit before we know that we have what is both necessary and sufficient.

How can you say everything about a problem and its solution that needs to be said without being too wordy? To begin with I admonish students not to leave anything out until their vocabulary and skills are developed well enough to produce an elegant write-up. It is a writing goal for mathematics and a reminder of the need for careful attention to the continuous development of a more sophisticated mathematics vocabulary. The ability to choose appropriate terminology is key to an elegant presentation.

GENERAL RUBRIC
Mathematics Problem-Solving Write-Up

Exemplary (6)
- ◆ Complete response with clear, elegant explanation
- ◆ Communicates to the intended audience with mature and accurate use of appropriate mathematics vocabulary
- ◆ Includes diagram or table
- ◆ Shows understanding of the mathematics ideas and processes
- ◆ Identifies important elements
- ◆ Presents strong arguments for the solution(s) with examples
- ◆ Generalizes the solution to related situations
- ◆ Generally goes beyond the expectations for the problem

Competent (5)
- ◆ Fairly complete response with clear explanations but says more than needed
- ◆ Communicates to the intended audience with good use of appropriate vocabulary
- ◆ May include diagram or table
- ◆ Shows understanding of the math ideas and processes
- ◆ Identifies important elements
- ◆ Presents solution(s) with solid arguments

Satisfactory with minor flaws (4)
- ◆ Completes problem satisfactorily
- ◆ Explanation muddled—some appropriate use of math term
- ◆ Arguments incomplete
- ◆ Diagram or table unclear
- ◆ Understands and uses the math ideas

Nearly satisfactory (3)
- ◆ Begins but does not complete the problem
- ◆ Does not show full understanding of the math ideas and processes
- ◆ Misuse or non-use of math terms
- ◆ Computational errors
- ◆ May use inappropriate strategy

FIGURE 4–2   *General Rubric Used as a Guide for Problem-Solving Write-Ups*

> **Incomplete (2)**
> - ◆ Starts
> - ◆ Explanation hard to understand
> - ◆ Diagram or table unclear
> - ◆ Does not understand the problem situation
> - ◆ Computational errors
>
> **Inadequate (1)**
> - ◆ Drawings or words do not reflect the problem
> - ◆ Copies part of the problem with no solution attempted
>
> **No attempt (0)**

FIGURE 4–2 *continued.*

Conducting a Peer Review

Before the problem-solving write-ups are submitted, students share their writing with their partners. Using the general rubric as a guide, each student makes comments and suggestions on the sticky notes affixed to the partner's paper. I remind them to be especially aware of the use of vocabulary. I become a consultant, helping as unobtrusively as possible. After the papers are returned to the writers, we set aside time for making revisions.

In many instances students want to make changes not because of a partner's suggestions but because of what they noticed in their partner's write-up. Sometimes students ask whether they can just start over. I consider individual requests and the reasons behind them. Generally, however, I want to see what they have already written so that I will be able to properly evaluate what they've rewritten. It's all about learning the mathematics, *using the language,* and learning how to learn. When I see those things happening, students get well-deserved positive feedback and support.

After the peer reviews have been completed, we talk about the solutions and thinking processes a bit more before I collect the write-ups. I review them and give the students additional feedback when I return the papers and have the students insert them into their binders.

I am always pleasantly surprised to find that my seventh and eighth graders use the concept of elegance as a beacon guiding them in the dark. It consistently shows up on their sticky-note comments when they review their fellow students' problem-solving write-ups. Since elegance is easier to see in the work of others, keeping it in mind while evaluating someone else's work seems a necessary conceptual development before one's own math writing can become elegant. Margaret Biggerstaff and her colleagues have similarly observed (1994) that "as students look at others' work, they will begin to see a need for clearer communication about their strategies."

Two Interesting Problems

Two problems have proven to be particularly engaging to my middle-school students. I developed the first, An Exploration into Sums, based on a homework problem in the "Accentuate the Negative" unit from *Connected Mathematics* (81, item 14). By the time I assign this problem, my students have learned to graph in four quadrants as part of their study of integers and have also learned to write equations by looking at patterns in tables and graphs.

The quality of work my students produce typically amazes me. I am surprised at the level of sophistication many of them have developed in looking for and describing patterns. Their writing gives me a window into the depth of thinking triggered by this investigation. It seems that when students know they will need to communicate their ideas in writing, they pay closer attention to detail. In turn, this keeps them engaged in the exploration long enough to capture unexpected nuggets of mathematics.

Alexis' solution is shown in Figure 4–3. She restates the problem succinctly. In the description of her "ah ha" moment and the thought pattern

Alexis Kellner Becker

An Exploration into Sums

We had to name five pairs of numbers with a sum of –3, then plot those pairs of numbers on a coordinate grid. We then made a table, and discovered a pattern. We made a rule for this pattern. Then we repeated this process for the number +8. We recorded our observations and made predictions.

I plucked from the air five pairs of numbers that I knew had sums of –3: (–2, –1), (–4, 1), (2, –5), (–6, 3), and (4, –7). I then graphed these coordinate pairs. The graph was linear and it crossed through –3. I made a mental note of this and went on. (See graph.)

After that, I made my table. My table looked like this:

X	Y
–3	0
–2	–1
–1	–2
0	–3
1	–4
2	–5
3	–6
4	–7

I noted that each time the X-variable increased by 1, the Y-variable decreased by 1. Then I tried to find my rule.

I tried first to find my rule from a pattern in the graph. At this I failed miserably. Then I stood back and took a good look at what I was doing, and the obvious answer popped into my head.

Obviously, if –3 is the sum of X + Y, then –3 = X + Y. Knowing that addition and subtraction are inverse operations, I figured that –3 – X = Y. Then, of course, Y = –3 – X. I checked it on my graphing calculator, and knew that I had the correct answer.

For +8, or any other number, it's basically the same. In a problem like this, n being the sum: Y = n – X.

I then took a closer look at my graphs, for –3 and +8. Both were linear and, as I mentioned before, both crossed through the given sum on both axes. This is because, if you're graphing the addends of a certain number, two points would be (n, 0) and (0, n).

This applies to any and all integer sums.

A possible extension would be to do the same problem, except with pairs of numbers with the difference of a given number. I think the results would be comparable, but with a twist.

FIGURE 4–3 *Alexis' Problem-Solving Write-Up for an Exploration Into Sums*

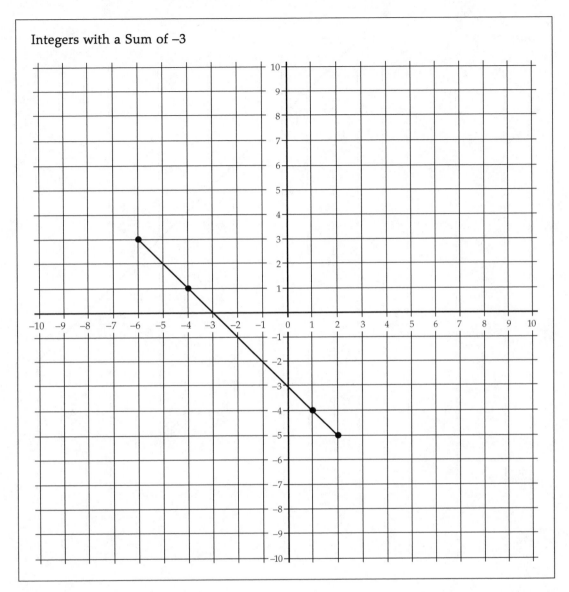

FIGURE 4–3   *continued.*

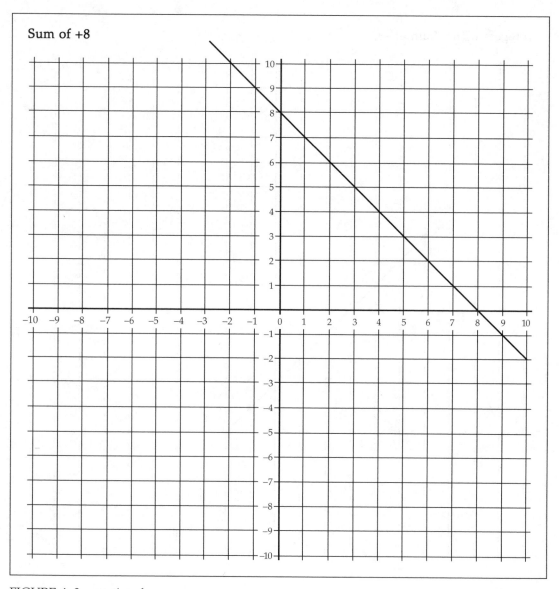

Sum of +8

FIGURE 4–3   *continued.*

Growing in Four Steps Write-Up

In this problem, there were two steps. In the first step, we had to find a number that will grow 10 into 20. To make the 10 grow, we had to multiply it by the same number four times. For example, if I chose the number 1.5, I would multiply (10 by 1.5) four times. The next step is to change the starting number from 10 to 16, and the ending number from 20 to 32. We then had to find the number that would grow 16 to 32.

To solve the first step, I used a guess and check method. I started with 1.2 because I knew that 2 would grow 10 way too large, and 1 would make it stay the same. These are my results for each step (this table shows every step of multiplication and the target that I want to reach).

Factor	Step 1	Step 2	Step 3	Step 4	Target
1.2	12	14.4	17.28	20.736	20

I then saw that this number was too high. I then continued to narrow it down by seeing if the number was too high or low, and if there were no more possibilities left in that place value, I moved one to the right. The number that I came up with is 1.189207115. This number grows 10 exactly to 20 accurate to 8 decimal places. Here is the table that shows the number and its steps.

Factor	Step 1	Step 2	Step 3	Step 4	Target
1.189207115	11.89207115	14.14213562	16.8179283	20	20

I then had the first step of the problem done, so I moved on to the second step. The first number that I tried was 1.189207115, the same number that grew 10 to 20 because I thought that it might work. It did grow 16 to 32. Here is the table showing this.

Factor	Step 1	Step 2	Step 3	Step 4	Target
1.189207115	19.02731384	22.627417	26.90868529	32	32

FIGURE 4–4 *Tyler's Problem-Solving Write-Up for Growing in Four Steps*

When I saw that 1.189207115 worked for both 10 to 20 and 16 to 32, I began to see a pattern. I had seen that both of the ending numbers were double the starting number. I then tried 1.189207115 with other starting numbers. I found that the ending number was always double the starting number. Then, with help from my math teacher, I, and other classmates noticed this. If you write an equation of the problem ($10n^4 = 20$, $n = 1.189207115$) you can replace n^4 with 2 ($10*2 = 20$). This would mean that $n^4 = 2$. I tried 1.189207115^4 and got an answer of 2. This means that when I was multiplying 10 and 16 by 1.189207115 four times, I was really multiplying them by 2.

A related problem could have the number quadruple instead of double.

FIGURE 4–4   *continued.*

that produced it, you can see the significant use of technical mathematics vocabulary: *coordinate pairs, linear, graph, rule, sum, inverse, operations, addends,* and *integer.* Her write-up is brief and to the point—it is elegant.

Many students rate Growing in Four Steps their favorite problem for the year. (I first saw this problem written up by Kris Acquarelli in an early *Math Solutions Newsletter.*) To solve this problem, students use a calculator to help them find a number they can multiply by, four consecutive times, starting with 10, in order to produce a product of 20. They then repeat the process, this time changing 16 to 32 in four consecutive multiplications by the same number. Tyler's write-up (see Figure 4–4) reveals a student beginning with a simple arithmetic process and independently thinking his way into the discovery of a highly sophisticated mathematical concept. He describes his insights with the ideal combination of vocabulary and symbolic representation. Notice, too, how Tyler has included his collaboration with others as well as his consultation with me. His document is a combination of significant ingredients that effect powerful mathematics learning and communication.

Conclusion

I use problem-solving write-ups at least once a month. It is an invaluable classroom ritual that reinforces the benefits of communicating mathematical thinking and ideas. Students give it high marks in their list of what helps them learn mathematics. They love exploring interesting and challenging problems and appreciate the opportunity to use vocabulary in meaningful ways. The write-ups give them a sense of accomplishment in situations where they are in charge of their own learning.

CHAPTER 5

Mathematical Reflections

Children do not learn by doing. . . . They learn by think-
ing, discussing, *and* reflecting *on what they have done.*
—WILLIAM SPEER (NCSM, 1997, II-H-16)

Reflection, whether or not it is set up formally, is an important component of any mathematics program. It pushes students to connect their
conceptual mathematical understanding to technical language by:

1. Using vocabulary and description.
2. Developing and using a rubric.
3. Participating in peer evaluation.
4. Using examples and illustrations to clarify meaning.

Teachers then use any awkward or incorrect summaries to plan follow-up
minilessons.

I organize my middle-level mathematics program around "investigations," as set out in *Connected Mathematics*. Every investigation consists of

a series of problems, each with follow-up and homework, designed to develop a big mathematical idea. At the end of each investigation, a "mathematical reflection"—a series of questions and prompts—guides students through a summary of key aspects of the mathematics they have learned. The entire class examines and discusses these items thoroughly, taking notes all the while. In their summary, the students use their notes—which should include key vocabulary and input from the teacher and classmates—as well as their own interpretations.

Overall, mathematical reflections are a multipurpose tool for learning and using technical terms and building and understanding essential mathematics. They encompass both review and assessment; they provide insight into individual student concept development and evaluative reasoning; and they help students develop their vocabulary and communication skills—all in one compact routine.

Learning to Use Mathematical Reflections

During the first year of my new math program, I struggled with how to structure the reflection process to best support my students. The following prompts are from the mathematical reflection for investigation 2 (analyzing data in tables, graphs, and written reports) of the Variables and Patterns *Connected Mathematics* unit:

1. What are the advantages and disadvantages of a table?
2. What are the advantages and disadvantages of a graph?
3. What are the advantages and disadvantages of a written report? Think about your answers to these questions, discuss your ideas with other students and your teacher, and then write a summary of your findings in your journal. *(35)*

In our discussion we talked extensively about the challenges of using data given in one form of representation—table, graph, or narrative—to create the other two representations, and described how one might do this. In connection with graphs, we also talked about selecting scales for the axes, when and why you might draw lines to connect the points, and how to interpret a connected interval.

Nathan then wrote the following reflection:

The advantages of a table [are] that you have the plot points (coordinate pairs) right there in order. But the disadvantages are that with a graph you can see more clearly the changes and progress. With a graph you can see the most or least progress clearly. The disadvantage is you have to look hard to find the plot numbers or the individual coordinate pairs. The written report is good because you can take the notes of the report and make them into a table and graph. The disadvantage is you have to use the points from notes to make a table or make a graph to, let's say, see the most and least progress in a person's bike trip or something.

Emily wrote:

From investigation 2 I've learned the advantages and disadvantages of tables: You can get exact answers and numbers; it's very straightforward. But it's not very visual. Graph: You can glance at it and see where there are big gaps and small gaps, but it's harder to find exact numbers. Written report: You have it in paragraph form so you don't have all the information right in front of you. But you have a lot of helpful information written down so you can remember.

I've learned how to make a graph from a table and a table from a graph. Also to read notes and then make a table or graph from it. And what everything means in a table and graph and where it goes.

I consider both of these reflections satisfactory, but limited with regard to what they incorporate from the class discussion.

By the third year of the program, I had made many attempts to improve student responses, including writing several reflections collaboratively with the class. Nevertheless, their reflections still lacked substance. My students came to the rescue when they asked me for a general rubric for assessing the reflections.

We made creating the rubric a class project. Together we brainstormed a list of characteristics that needed to be demonstrated for a reflection to receive a check-plus rating (the highest rating).

Prioritized, our list was:

1. must be in summary form
2. includes all responses to the questions
3. connects the different concepts of the investigation
4. shows understanding of all math concepts in the investigation
5. correct use of vocabulary words
6. uses examples and illustrations
7. uses charts and tables as needed
8. the writing is elegant
9. neatly written

A discussion about *elegant* as a criterion brought us to the conclusion that it wouldn't serve the purpose of a reflection, which is to bring out all possible perspectives on the big mathematical idea or concepts being developed in the investigation. With a little tweaking, we then came up with the following general rubric:

Characteristics for a Check-Plus Rating

◆ The reflection is written in summary form.

◆ All concepts explored in the investigation are included.

◆ All responses to the prompts (questions) are included in the summary.

◆ Examples and illustrations are included to clarify arguments and explanations.

◆ Charts, tables, and graphs are used when appropriate.

◆ Appropriate vocabulary is used accurately.

◆ Calculations and estimations are reasonable and/or accurate.

Marcia's reflection below demonstrates the dramatic improvement that was evident across the board once this rubric had been established:

In this investigation we analyzed data that was given in written notes and reports, tables and graphs that were on a bike ride of the day. Each character would take notes, make a table or a graph of how far the friends rode that day. We explored the advantages and disadvantages of each of these things.

Advantages to a Graph:

1. You can see the jumps easier from one point to another.

2. You can connect the points to see what happens between the points.

3. It's more visual; you don't have to concentrate very hard.

Disadvantages:

1. You don't get exact numbers.

2. Have to find a good scale for each axis.

3. Sometimes points are hard to plot.

4. Hard to create notes or report from a day's work.

Advantages to a Table:

1. Gives exact numbers and data.

2. Easy to create.

3. Can find difference between intervals.

Disadvantages:

1. Not as visual as a graph.

2. Harder to spot patterns.

3. Have to work to read the data.

Advantages to a Written Report or Notes:

1. You can combine the graph and the table in the report.

2. Can give you the exact numbers and the two variables.

3. Doesn't take work to read.

Disadvantages:

1. Hard to make a graph or table from notes.

2. Most of the time doesn't give exact data.

In this investigation we also had to make graphs from tables and visa versa as well as make written reports from tables and graphs and make tables and graphs from notes on the day's ride. We learned how to do each of these things. It was easiest for me to make a graph from a table because all the information was given, including the two variables. I found it hardest to create a graph from notes because there was no exact data given and very few boundaries. I think this whole investigation was good review on plotting points and a good lesson on how to create things (that were relatively correct) from little data.

Peer Review

As with all our mathematics writing activities, reflections undergo a peer review. Using the rubric as guide, each student reads his or her partner's reflection, writes comments and suggestions on sticky notes, and returns it for last-minute revisions. In most instances students also assign a rating to the writing. I ask students to leave the sticky notes on the papers when they are submitted. The notes provide added information for me about the readers' reactions to the reflections and their attention to detail. (See Figure 5–1). The comments are seldom insightful, but the students are generally kind and positive, pay attention to the various expected elements, and are prompted to think about their own attempts to communicate mathematically in writing. The ratings are always in the check-plus or nearly check-plus categories (or, otherwise, blank).

Sometimes a student will do a more thorough analysis. First, here's Peter's reflection on understanding *surface area* and *volume* in rectangular prisms:

> In this investigation we explored rectangular boxes and we made flat patterns for boxes. We found the dimensions of a box, the total area of all its faces, and the number of unit cubes required to fill it.
>
> If you were a packaging engineer you would want to know the total area of all the faces so you knew how much material you needed to wrap it.
>
> To find the area of all the faces of a rectangular box, you add the area of all the faces. But since it's a rectangular box you can add the area of all the different faces and multiply it by two, because on a

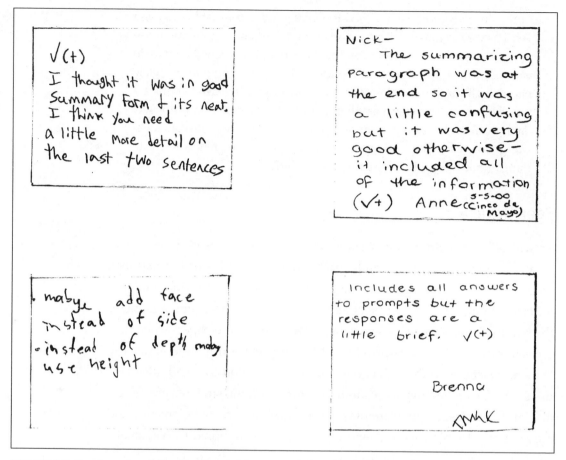

FIGURE 5–1   *Samples of Peer Review Sticky Notes for Mathematical Reflections*

rectangular box there are always pairs of faces. The only exception is if all 4 sides of the rectangle are the same. To find the number of unit cubes needed to fill a rectangular box you find the volume: length × width × height.

A feature that must be the same for any flat pattern for a box is that they have the same surface area. A feature that could be different is the arrangement.

And Figure 5–2 is Nat's peer review.

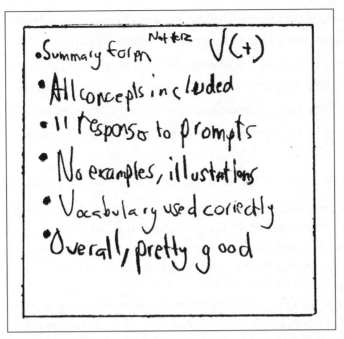

FIGURE 5–2   *Nat's Peer Review Sticky Note for Peter's Reflection on Understanding Surface Area and Volume for Rectangular Prisms*

Communicating Mathematically

Many of my students' mathematical reflections demonstrate that they are able to use complex mathematics vocabulary and provide informative concept descriptions. Investigations 2 and 3 of the *Connected Mathematics* unit on integer operations titled Accentuate the Negative involve the addition and subtraction of integers, explored through the use of chipboards, number lines, and patterns. The summary prompts are:

1. Write a strategy for finding the difference of two integers. Be sure to consider all possible combinations of positive integers, negative integers, and 0. Verify your strategy by finding the following differences.

$$5 - 9 \qquad {}^-5 - {}^+3 \qquad {}^-5 - {}^-3 \qquad 5 - {}^-9$$

2. Without actually calculating the sum, how can you decide if the sum of two integers is positive? negative? zero?

3. Without actually calculating the difference, how can you decide if the difference of two integers is positive? negative? zero?

4. Describe how addition and subtraction of integers are related.

5. Describe how to find the absolute value of any number.

Here's Alexis' reflection:

Finding the difference of two positive integers is simple: simply subtract one from the other. For example: +70 − +64 = +6. If the subtrahend is of greater absolute value than the minuend, simply do the same thing, but your difference will be negative: +3 − +5 = −2; 5 − 9 = −4. You go left on the number line.

Subtracting negative numbers is the same as adding positive numbers. For example: −5 − −3 = −2 and −5 + +3 = −2. You go right on the number line.

A negative number minus a positive number would be the same as adding a negative number, going left on the number line: −5 − +3 = −8.

Subtracting a negative from a positive number is the same as adding a positive number, going right on the number line: +5 − −9 = +14.

Any integer subtracted from zero, keeps its absolute value, but becomes negative if it was positive, and vice versa. For example: 0 − −4 = +4; 0 − +4 = −4.

The sum of two integers is positive if both of the numbers are over 0 or one is zero and the other is positive, or if one is positive and it is of greater absolute value than the negative. The sum is negative if both of the numbers are negative, one is 0 and the other is negative, or if one is a negative and is of greater absolute value than the positive. The sum is 0 when a positive is added to a negative of the same absolute value, or vice versa or if the problem is 0 + 0.

The difference of a positive minuend and negative subtrahend is always positive, and the difference of a negative minuend and a positive subtrahend is always negative. The difference of two positive numbers is negative if the subtrahend is of greater absolute value than the minuend, and positive if it is of lesser absolute value. The same applies to negative numbers in reverse. An integer subtracted by itself equals 0.

Addition and subtraction are inverse operations: one undoes the other.

The absolute value of a number is its distance from 0 on a number line. In addition to counting on a number line, a simpler way to figure the absolute value of any number is that the number itself is its own absolute value. For example: the absolute value of +6 is 6; and the absolute value of –50 is 50.

Alexis sets the record for effective repeated and meaningful use of key technical terminology related to a single concept! If the rubric had incorporated the elegance characteristic, Alexis would not likely have been so thorough in describing each possible case for adding and subtracting integers. Not only did she need to think carefully while composing the reflection, I had to think as carefully when reading it. I found myself reading, rereading, and testing each of her statements for confirmation and accuracy. In addition, Alexis sprinkled examples generously throughout the reflection.

The investigation on maximum and minimum surface areas and volume (Filling and Wrapping, *Connected Mathematics*) concludes with these summary prompts:

1. For a given number of cubes, what arrangement will give a rectangular prism with the least surface area? What arrangement will give a rectangular prism with the greatest surface area? Use specific examples to illustrate your ideas.
2. Describe how you can find the surface area of a rectangular prism.
3. What is the relationship between the number of unit cubes needed to fill a prism-shaped box and the volume of the box?
4. Describe how you can find the volume of any prism.

Ceysa's reflection (see Figure 5–3) exemplifies the effective use of illustrations and vocabulary even though she struggles with spelling. Her examples are neatly clarified with sketches. Note especially her description of *volume*, where she shows the count of the cubes inside with meticulous labeling. Ceysa has used all the tools available to communicate her mathematical

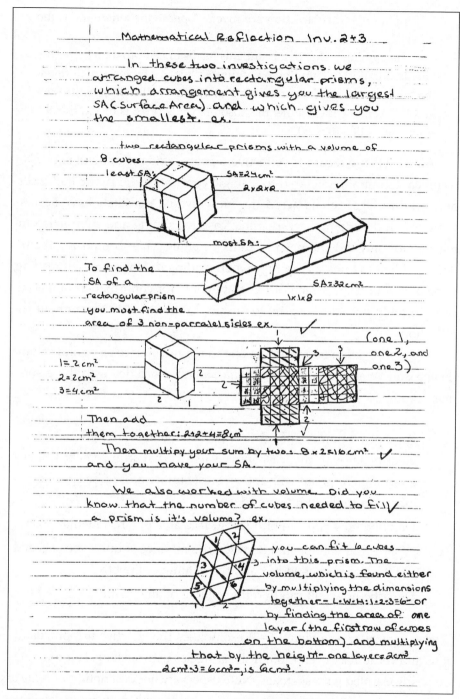

Mathematical Reflection Inv. 2+3

In these two investigations we arranged cubes into rectangular prisms, which arrangement gives you the largest SA (Surface Area) and which gives you the smallest. ex.

two rectangular prisms with a volume of 8 cubes.

least SA:
SA=24cm²
2x2x2 ✓

most SA:
SA=32cm²
1x1x8

To find the SA of a rectangular prism you must find the area of 3 non-parralel sides ex. ✓

(one 1, one 2, and one 3)

1=2 cm²
2=2 cm²
3=4 cm²

Then add them together: 2+2+4=8cm²

Then multiply your sum by two: 8x2=16cm² ✓ and you have your SA.

We also worked with volume. Did you know that the number of cubes needed to fill a prism is it's volume? ex.

you can fit 6 cubes into this prism. The volume, which is found either by multiplying the dimensions together - L·W·H:1·2·3=6 - or by finding the area of one layer (the first row of cubes on the bottom) and multiplying that by the height- one layer: 2cm³ 2cm³·3=6cm³, is 6cm³.

FIGURE 5–3 *Ceysa's Reflection on Surface Area and Volume for Rectangular Prisms Showing the Effective Use of Illustration and Vocabulary*

ideas clearly—technical language, selected examples, and carefully executed illustrations in an organized presentation.

Evaluating Mathematical Statements

My students usually have the most difficulty using mathematical language in describing patterns. This is most pronounced in our introductory work on integer operations. After working with two different models—positive and negative chips representing zero, and the number line—students appear comfortable doing the computations. But it's a totally different picture when they attempt to describe what they are doing in writing. (The careful work of Alexis, shown earlier, is the exception, not the rule!)

The following excerpts from various student reflections prompted a minilesson on writing and evaluating accurate mathematical statements:

◆ A strategy for finding the difference of two integers is if the symbols are the same just use normal subtraction.

◆ When a positive is being subtracted from a negative, ignore all symbols and add the two numbers; then put a negative symbol in front of the difference.

◆ When the subtrahend and the minuend are opposite numbers (meaning they have the same absolute value) the difference will be zero.

◆ When a negative is being subtracted from a positive, it's just like subtracting positives.

◆ If the minuend is larger than the subtrahend the difference will have the symbol of the minuend.

◆ You can find the difference between two negative integers by just subtracting the values.

Mathematical Reflection (Inv. 3)

In this investigation we learned how to ⟶ AN
subtract two integers. We used chip boards and number
lines to help us. We learned that subtracting a number
is the same as adding it's opposite. For example
5-9=⁻4. (5+⁻9=⁻4), ⁻5-⁺3= ⁻8 (⁻5+⁻3=⁻8), ⁻5-⁻3=⁻2
(⁻5+⁺3=⁻2), and 5-⁻9=14 (5+9=14).

In a subtraction problem the difference is positive
when the minuend is greater than the subtrahend.
For example ⁺5-⁻2=⁺7. The difference is negative
when the subtrahend is greater than the minuend.
ex. ⁻4-6=⁻10.

Adding and subtracting integers are inverse
opperations. When you add you do the oppsite of what
you would do when you are subtracting. For example
if you were adding 5 and 8, on a number line you
would go five places to the right, and then eight
more places to the right and end up at 13. Where
as if you were subtracting you would go five places
to the right, and then eight places to the left and
end up at ⁻3.

To find the absolute value of any number you
find the distance between it and zero on a number
line. An easier way to think about this is to just
ignore any signs it has. For example the absolute value
of ⁻16 is 16, the absolute value of 184 is 184. The
symbol for absolute value is |.| with the number
inside (|2|, or |⁻8|). |⁻28|=28° is read the absolute value
of ⁻28 is 28. So |2|=2 and |⁻8|=8.

FIGURE 5–4 *Ruthie's Reflection on Adding and Subtracting Integers, Used to Model Critical Proofreading With Particular Attention to the Accurate Use of Technical Vocabulary*

We analyzed each statement according to the following prompts:

1. Is the statement true?
2. How do you know?
3. Find an example or a counterexample.
4. If it is true, is it useful or helpful?
5. If it is not true, could you change it fairly easily (a word or two) to make it true?

First, we read each statement as a class. Then table partners applied the prompts to the statement and came up with examples or counterexamples to justify their conclusion. Partners shared their ideas, and when appropriate the statement was reworded and students recorded the refined and proven statement. Finally the class discussed usefulness—did the statement represent a clear procedure for computing with integers?

We finished the lesson with some practice proofreading, using Ruthie's reflection (see Figure 5–4) on the overhead. Ruthie is able to keep it all straight and express her understanding in clear and precise language with good examples. We read the reflection together and checked each example for alignment with the preceding statement. For example, for Ruthie's first statement ("subtracting a number is the same as adding its opposite"), I asked, "What opposites are subtracted and added?" "What is meant by *is the same as*?" "Make up another example of your own."

A lesson like this gives all students a model for carefully examining mathematical statements. It relies heavily on knowing vocabulary, thinking and reasoning about how statements can be exemplified, and providing convincing evidence of understanding. In many instances this means examining a range of numbers in order to assure a consistent pattern to match the statement.

CHAPTER 6

Expanding Vocabulary with Journals and Homework

*The chief merit of language is clearness, and we know that
nothing detracts so much from this as do unfamiliar terms.*
—GALEN (A.D. 129–199)

Remember that the three-ring binder around which my math class is
organized is introduced during the first week of school. At that time
students learn how to use each section of the binder to keep track of
the work they do.

Journals

The student journal is the first section of the binder. In it, each student re-
sponds to the mathematics he or she encounters in class during the year.
There are clear guidelines for using the student journal.

> Your *journal* is the first section of your binder. You will record your math
> work in it every day, to include the following:

◆ All work you do for in-class problems. Include words, charts, pictures, diagrams, or anything else to *show your thinking.*

◆ Any notes that you take during minilessons or class dialogues. Write anything that will help you remember what you are thinking and that you can refer back to for help.

◆ Your daily math reflections. Write a summary of the math concepts and ideas encountered during math class. Include new understanding you have developed, questions you have about the topic, and connections you can make to other areas of math or other subjects.

◆ To help keep your journal organized please:

Date every entry and identify problems you are working on with titles, investigation and problem numbers, and unit names when appropriate.

Label your daily reflection.

Start each day with a note about beginnings and warm-ups.

I explain that the journal is like a personal textbook to be used as a reference throughout their work on the current unit, and beyond.

I then clarify each element in these guidelines, displaying and sharing earlier student work as concrete examples of how the journal should be used. I use both hard copies and overhead transparencies, because some students need to touch the work and see it up close while I highlight specifics on the overhead. Audrey's journal pages (see Figure 6–1) show how a full day's classwork might be tracked. She records new vocabulary and uses sketches to help her remember meanings. She notes how the day began, records the work in class finding ratios of corresponding lengths for similar figures, and finally summarizes the day's highlights in her daily reflection.

The sample from Brenna's journal (see Figure 6–2) shows a portion of her record of finding the areas and perimeters of eight different triangles that were presented on a grid background with various orientations (the problems are from the Covering and Surrounding unit of *Connected Mathematics*). She explains the process she used for determining each area and

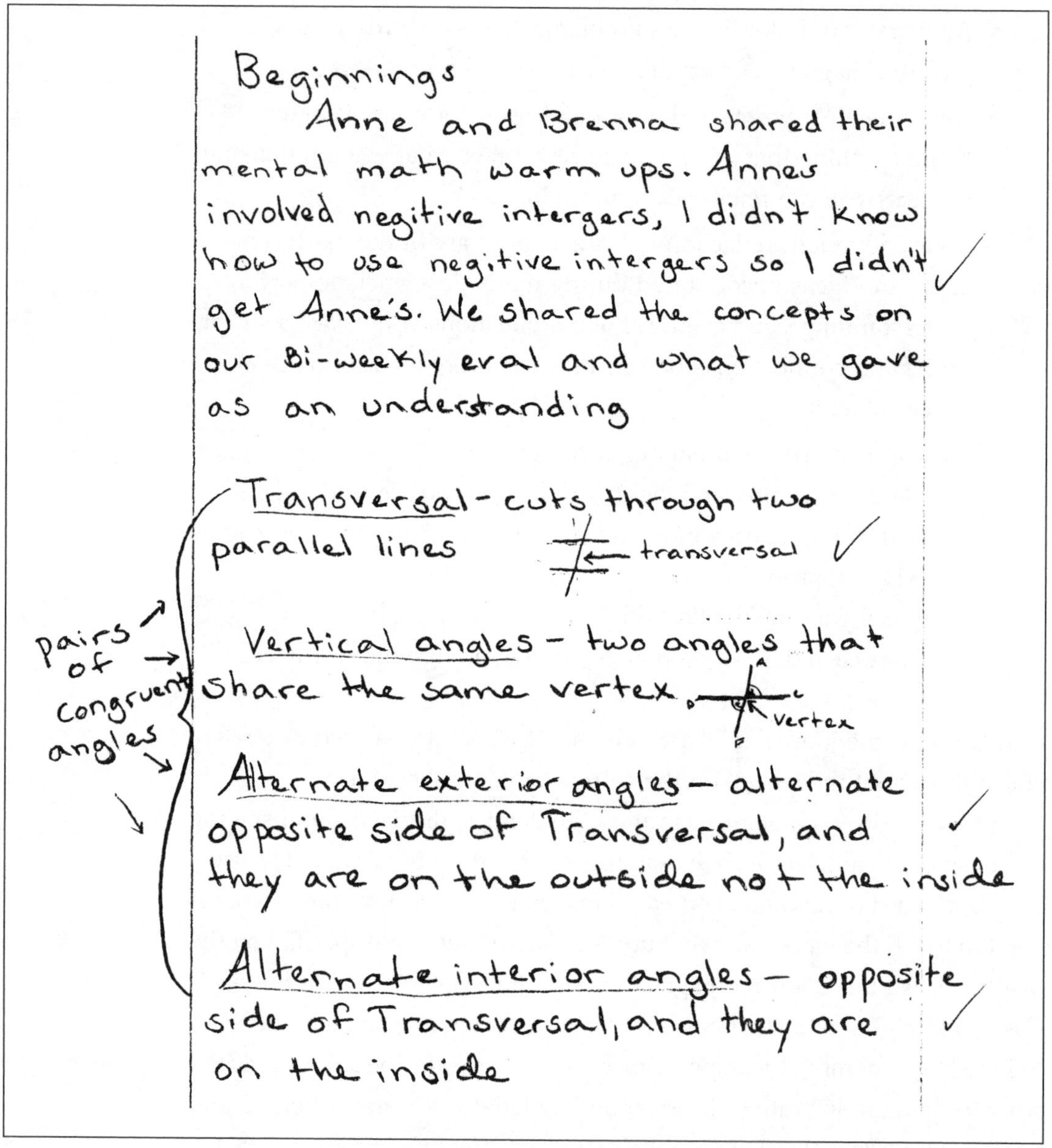

Beginnings
    Anne and Brenna shared their mental math warm ups. Anne's involved negitive intergers, I didn't know how to use negitive intergers so I didn't get Anne's. We shared the concepts on our Bi-weekly eval and what we gave as an understanding ✓

Transversal - cuts through two parallel lines   ⟶ transversal ✓

pairs of congruent angles →

Vertical angles - two angles that share the same vertex. ⟶ vertex

Alternate exterior angles - alternate opposite side of Transversal, and they are on the outside not the inside ✓

Alternate interior angles - opposite side of Transversal, and they are on the inside ✓

FIGURE 6–1   *Two Pages From Audrey's Journal Recording Work for an Entire Class Period From the Beginnings to the Daily Reflection*

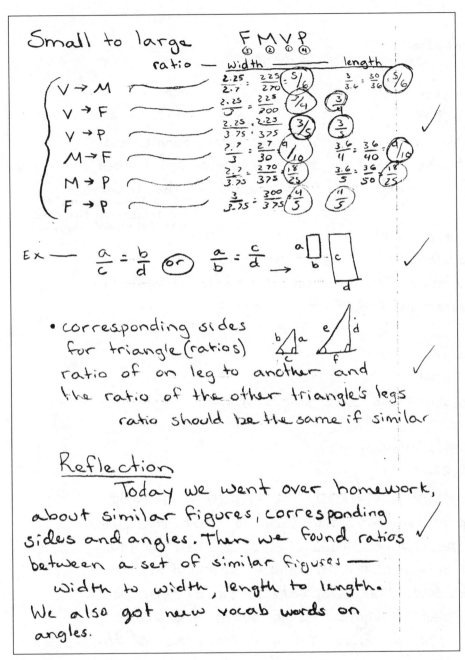

Small to large   F M V P
                   ③ ② ① ④
          ratio — width _____ length

V → M   2.25 : 225 = 5/6   3 : 30 = 5/6
         2.7   270   3.6 36

V → F   2.25 = 225 = 3/4   3 = 3/4
         3   300   4

V → P   2.25 : 2.25 = 3/5   3 = 3/5
         3.75   375   5

M → F   2.7 = 27 = 9/10   3.6 : 36 = 9/10
         3   30   4   40

M → P   2.7 : 270 = 18/25   3.6 = 36 = 18/25
         3.75 375   5   50

F → P   3 : 300 = 4/5   1/5
         3.75 375

Ex —   a/c = b/d (or) a/b = c/d → [a b] [c d]

• corresponding sides
  for triangle (ratios)
  ratio of on leg to another and
  the ratio of the other triangle's legs
        ratio should be the same if similar

Reflection

        Today we went over homework,
about similar figures, corresponding
sides and angles. Then we found ratios
between a set of similar figures —
        width to width, length to length.
We also got new vocab words on
angles.

FIGURE 6–1   continued.

Invest.6/6.1

A. Perimeter - 17u
   Area - 12u²
   Explanation - I made it into a rectangle and
   found the area of the rectangle and figured
   half of that was the area of the triangle.
                                    I found the perimeter
                                    by measuring the sides
                                    and adding them together.

B. Perimeter - 29 u
   Area - 35u²
   Explanation - The same way I did A for both the
   Perimeter and Area.

C. Perimeter - 19½ u
   Area - 12u²
   Explanation - The same way I did A.

D. Perimeter - 24¼ u
   Area - 27u²
   Explanation - I broke up the triangle so I could
   make rectangles around them so that the peice
   of the triangle obviosly filled up half so you
   could measure the rectangle and split it in
   half and that was the area of the peice
   of that triangle so I added the area
   of the 2 peices to get the area of the
   triangle. For the perimeter I meaured all
   the sides and added them together.

FIGURE 6–2 *Brenna's Journal Record of Her Work on Problem 6.1 From the Covering and Surrounding Unit of* Connected Mathematics

perimeter. (At this point in the year, students have not yet developed formulas for finding the area and perimeter of a triangle.)

When I display these examples, I ask my students to identify the important journal guideline elements that are being represented. I also point out how the journal is an opportunity to practice using appropriate mathematics vocabulary. It is a good time to remind them that a strong vocabulary is built from understanding what the words mean and using them repeatedly in meaningful ways. I never let up on that message.

Figure 6–3 is an example of Brenna's notes taken during a minilesson on the relationships between volumes and surface areas of cylinders, spheres, and cones. Notice how she has used vocabulary related to symbolic representations. As her teacher, I am aware that she has not included sketches with her notes, and perhaps she didn't need to. But because I know the lesson was centered on concrete models, I point this out, driving home

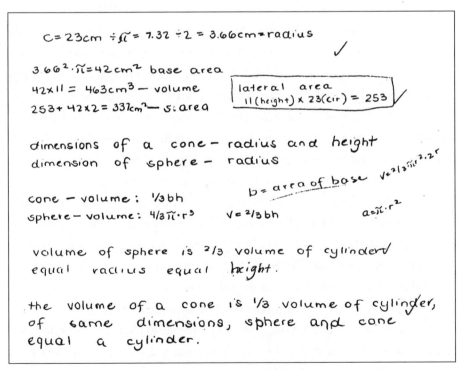

FIGURE 6–3 *Brenna's Notes on the Relationships Between Volumes and Surface Areas for Cylinders, Spheres, and Cones*

that illustrations are important in clarifying and developing concepts. I also return to Audrey's complete journal page and remind students of her effective use of sketches.

The daily math reflection has proven to be one of the most difficult rituals for me to implement. The idea of summarizing mathematical *thinking* is new to many students, and they are easily drawn down the lazy pathway. At most they are willing to "log" the activities of the day. It is a huge challenge to get students to verbalize about the mathematics they've learned or used rather than simply list the problem numbers and/or titles (in essence, repeating my lesson plan). However, listing doesn't require thinking, so I hound them, celebrating the good examples I find. Eventually the daily reflections improve. It also helps when students begin to understand how the procedure helps them in the long run. The reflections are opportunities to use mathematics vocabulary in meaningful contexts as well as good learning records that help them complete the self-evaluations required every two weeks.

I show students several examples of successful approaches to fulfilling the math reflection requirement. Tyler's entry (see Figure 6–4) is a basic, good-quality example of a daily reflection. Brenna's (see Figure 6–5) is more detailed. She does list problem numbers but is careful to talk about the mathematics involved in each of the class segments. Tyler's and Brenna's reflections are especially notable because they indicate insights they experienced while doing the work. In addition, Brenna always comments about her perceived level of ease or difficulty with each challenge.

As we look carefully at the examples of daily reflections, I ask students to find instances of the qualities expected in a daily mathematical reflection: new understanding, questions about the topic, and connections to other mathematics or subjects. I also ask them to point out how mathematics vocabulary is being used in meaningful ways.

Special class-time assignments are also recorded in the journal. For example, near the end of each trimester, in preparation for completing the self-evaluations for their portfolios, students make a list of what they have learned during the trimester (see Ethan's list in Figure 6–6). As you can see, use of technical vocabulary is again essential—more practice!

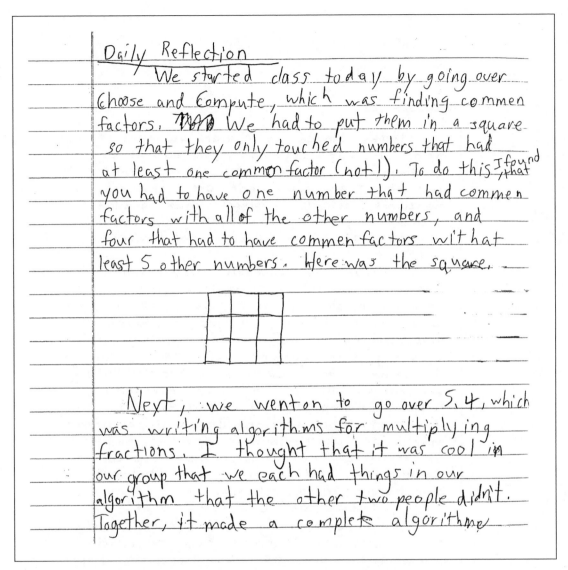

FIGURE 6–4 *A Typical Daily Math Reflection From Tyler's Journal*

The final guidelines deal with conventions. Again, we review examples
on the overhead, hammering away at the organizational details that will
make *all of our lives* easier.

Inevitably, I need to check student journals and give the feedback essential to steady progress and improvement. I certainly don't collect all those
binders! (Can you imagine the "ape arms" I would develop hauling them

vocab
isometric area
surface area
volumes
Faces
virtex
cube
rectangular prizm

Reflection

Today Marcia did her warm-up
and I was off by 1, I add too
quickly and it messed up my final
answer. Then we went over the ACE
homework which involved making flat
patterns for boxes which gave me
trouble at first but I got better
at it.

Then we finished Investigation
One (1.3 and 1.4). 1.3 involved finding
the dimensions of a closed box
and then finding a flat patterns
and cutting it to match - I had trouble
creating the pattern but once I had
a pattern the cutting was easy. Then
we moved on to 1.4 which gave you
3 flat patterns and you had to find its
dimensions and volume and surface area -
this was pretty simple and it helped
us realize the relationship between
dimensions and s. area and between
dimensions and volume.

Then we started Invest 2.
2.1 was something we did at family
math but I learned how to draw
3-D figures on the isometric dot paper,
then we explored the relationship between
dimensions and surface area with a constant
volume - it confirmed my assumptions that
the closer the shape was to a cube the
smaller the surface area would be.

FIGURE 6–5   *A More Detailed Math Reflection From Brenna's Journal*

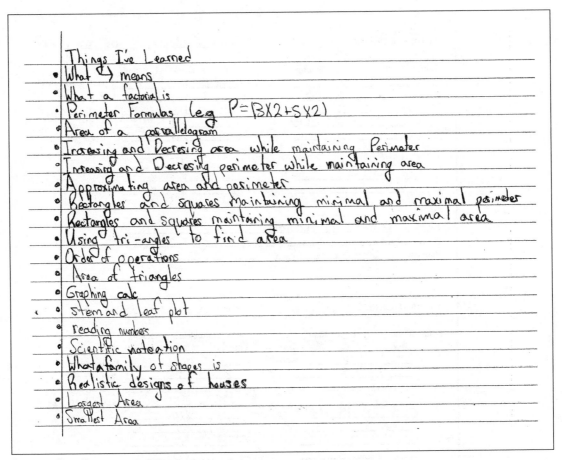

FIGURE 6–6 *Ethan's List of Learnings From His Trimester One Journal Record*

home?) Instead, each student has a "journal folder." Periodically I ask them to place their journal pages for specific dates into the folders, and I collect the folders. I have special forms on which I record my evaluation of their work (see Figure 6–7), and occasionally students fill out a duplicate self-evaluation so that we can compare our reactions. This is a significant opportunity for them to look at their own work from a more objective perspective. While evaluating the students' record keeping during a journal check I typically list areas of need for individuals and the class (see Figure 6–8). I then use the list as a guide for building suitable minilessons.

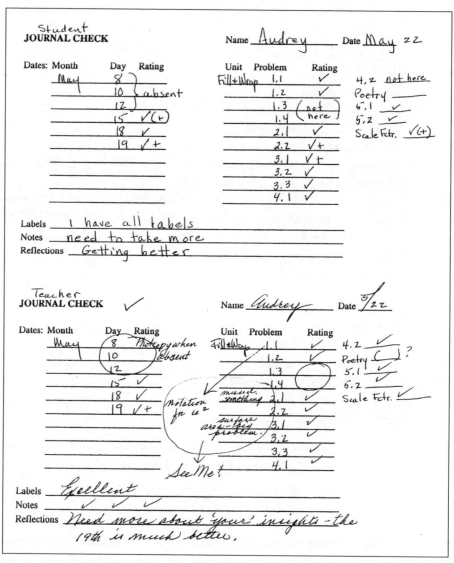

FIGURE 6–7 *Sample of a Completed Evaluation Form for the Monthly Journal Check; this one was completed by the student first, then the teacher.*

Homework

Next, we tackle homework. I designed the binder homework log after struggling with an irregular math schedule and with layering short- and long-term assignments. This format did wonders for student accountability. It is a clear, concrete, sequential record of what is assigned, when it is assigned,

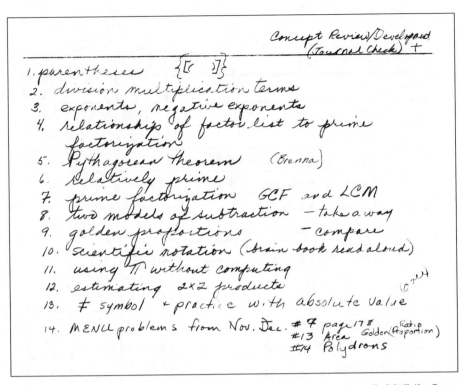

FIGURE 6–8 *My List of Notes About Concepts to Review, Compiled While Completing the Monthly Journal Check*

and when it is due. There is also space for students to track when they completed the assignment and when it was discussed in class and/or submitted to me for feedback. The homework log precedes all the binder's section dividers, so it is the first item visible when the binder is opened. Parents look at the form during the first parent meeting, and it substantially eases the home–school relationship. It is clear to everyone that the homework log is straightforward and doable and totally the student's responsibility. A page from the homework log is included in each trimester portfolio. Students highlight two assignments—the most challenging one and their favorite—and explain their choices. (A completed homework log is shown in Figure 6–9. There is usually more than one assignment for any single day.)

The homework assignments themselves almost always require explanations that provide opportunities to use technical vocabulary. The problems

green = fun
yellow = challenging
Homework Assignment Log for   Name Marcia

Date	Assignment	Date Due	Date completed	Date checked/ handed in
2·5·99	Self eval. 2·1 / 2·5	2·8·99	2·5·99	☆
2·5·99	Finish 5.2	2·8·99	2·5·99	☆
2·8·99	ACE 6,11,14 chipboard of # line	2·10·99	2·9·99	☆
2·8·99	3 games could help with	2·10·99	2·9·99	☆
2·8·99	5.3 and Follow-up	2·10·99	2·9·99	☆
2·10·99	Vocab and journal hand-in	2·12·99	2·10·99	☆
2·22·99	Math reflection page 82	2·26·99	2·25·99	☆
2·24·99	Vocabulary 90	2·26·99	2·24·99	☆
2·24·99	Question Bank 1-9	2·26·99	2·24·99	☆
2·26·99	Weekly Self eval.	3·1·99	2·26·99	☆
2·26·99	Parent letter signed	3·1·99	2·26·99	☆
3·1·99	Menu Problem write-ups	3·5·99	3·4·99	☆
3·3·99	Vocabulary 95	3·5·99	3·4·99	☆
3·3·99	Finish 1.2 and Follow-up	3·5·99	3·3·99	☆
3·5·99	ACE 1-14	3·8·99	3·7·99	☆
3·5·99	Self eval 3-1 / 3-5	3·8·99	3·7·99	☆
3·10·99	Math reflection p.15	3·12·99	3·11·99	☆
3·10·99	Vocabulary 100	3·12·99	3·10·99	☆
3·12·99	Self evaluation 3·8 / 3·12	3·15·99	3·12·99	☆
3·12·99	Finish 2.2	3·15·99	3·12·99	☆
3·12·99	Ace 1-8 and 17-22	3·15·99	3·14·99	☆

FIGURE 6–9   *A Completed Page From Marcia's Homework Log*

seldom ask for simple numerical answers; instead, they require descriptions, comparisons, or reasons. Zephyr's work in Figure 6–10 is typical and includes these characteristics.

Another type of homework is a reading response. For example, I typically give students an article to read and ask them to respond by writing a

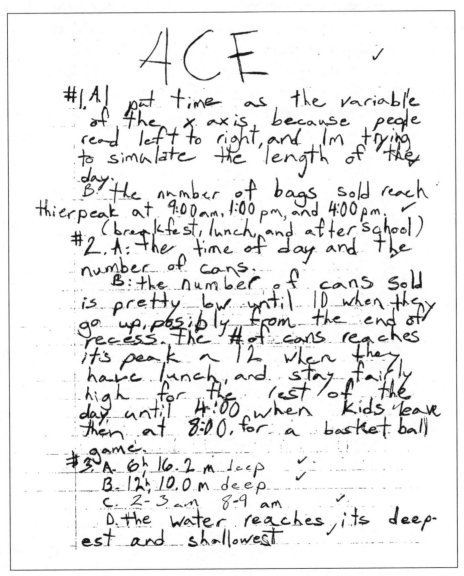

FIGURE 6–10 *Zephyr's Homework Illustrating the Explanations That Are Expected to Accompany Responses*

letter to the author of the article. Middle-school students are highly motivated when they are asked to read and respond to articles targeted to parents, teachers, or other adults.

At the beginning of the class I ask students to take out the previous evening's homework and share their results with their tablemates. If they have disagreements they are unable to resolve, the group then submits them to the class for consideration. I also choose some items that highlight significant vocabulary and mathematical development and share them with the whole class. Then the work is submitted for my review and feedback as appropriate to the assignment. My goals are to make best use of the time available and to give students more opportunities to communicate mathematically and learn from one another.

....

CHAPTER 7

Self-Assessment as a Vocabulary Development Tool

*The capability and willingness to assess their own
progress and learning is one of the greatest gifts students
can develop. . . . Mathematical power comes with knowing
how much we know and what to do to learn more.*
 —JEAN KERR STENMARK (1989, 26)

I have always used some form of self-evaluation with my students. In earlier years, this didn't receive a lot of positive reaction from my colleagues (nor did studying mathematics vocabulary, for that matter). Many of them felt having students do self-evaluations was a waste of time— kids simply told you what they thought you wanted to hear. But because those were the days of isolated classroom teaching, I went ahead without a collegial benediction and experienced the rewards of getting students more involved in their own learning.

Today, the literature presents in plentiful detail the reasons for instituting self-evaluation and self-assessment practices and the benefits gained in the process. In NCTM's *Mathematics Assessment* (1991), Jean Stenmark summarizes the value of student self-evaluation as promoting "metacognition skills, ownership of learning, and independence of thought" (55). Nancie

Atwell (1998) refers to her students as being "in a constant state of self-evaluation" as she strives to "put students' appraisals of their work at the heart of the evaluation process" (300–301).

Whatever choice teachers make for involving students in assessing and evaluating their own work, it pays off in rich dividends. It is a form of focused reflection that gives students the power to understand how they think, how they communicate, how they process information, and in essence how they learn. This is an important rung on the ladder to lifelong learning.

I use two self-assessment rituals in my classroom to enhance vocabulary acquisition. The first one, biweekly self-evaluations, is brief and is completed every two weeks. The second one, trimester self-evaluations, is much more detailed and comprehensive, and is completed at the end of each trimester.

Biweekly Self-Evaluations

Believing that learners have the most at stake in the evaluation process, I want them to play an active and significant role. Enter the five-item biweekly mathematics self-evaluation—a vital opportunity for the meaningful use of vocabulary and an instance of the student's being responsible for his or her learning. This regular biweekly self-evaluation also keeps students on their toes with regard to their daily journal entries.

The first prompt of this self-evaluation form directs students to review their work (classwork, homework, journal, and vocabulary) for a specified time period and list the mathematics concepts the class has studied. One purpose is to reinforce the value of record keeping. Another is to have them revisit and review their notes in order to appreciate themselves and the enormous amount of work they are doing. The third and most important purpose is that every time they name a concept, they are writing vocabulary.

The next prompt asks students to refer to their journals in order to evaluate their level of understanding and give an example as evidence of that understanding. I am most attentive to the response to this prompt when I review the assignment. A complete response worthy of a highly valued check-plus rating calls for the meaningful use of vocabulary if the student is to successfully present convincing evidence of current conceptual understanding.

Prompt number three asks students to check on homework and vocabulary, the fourth asks them to summarize new understanding and ask questions, and in the fifth and final segment students reflect on key elements of their effort and behavior.

I began with a weekly self-evaluation but quickly realized that every two weeks was more effective. Students receive a form on Friday that is due on Monday. The dates covered are written at the top of the form and entered on the homework log. On Monday, before the completed forms are submitted, I sweep through the class, asking them to list concepts until they have exhausted their collective litany. Students who may have overlooked something will scramble to add it to their list—great! It is also another opportunity to see and hear the terminology, a simple reinforcement that encourages full participation.

The greatest benefit from the routine (and there are many) is the golden opportunity to display and use the vocabulary that has been encountered during the two weeks. There is no doubt that Audrey, on the basis of the self-evaluation shown in Figure 7–1, has made the distributive property a part of her, mathematically speaking—it will never be forgotten, and if it is, she will be able to reconstruct it.

Audrey's presentation of evidence reminds me of Joan Countryman's astute observations about words as thinking tools and the hazards associated with words in mathematics, particularly if the focus is on definitions:

> Definitions alone rarely throw much light on the ideas they represent. They are usually the end product of much exploration and careful thought. In fact, the precision of a definition belies the effort that has contributed to its formulation. (1992, 55)

Blachowicz and Fisher, in *Teaching Vocabulary in All Classrooms* (1996), remind us of this as well:

Bi-weekly Mathematics Self-Evaluation   Grades 7 and 8

Name _Audrey_

Dates covered _10·25 — 11·5_

1. Summarize the mathematics concepts we have studied during the above time period. (list)

- adding/subtracting/multiplying/ dividing fractions
- F,D,P - memorize
- Dividing and multiplication
- algorithms on multiplying fractions

- relatively prime numbers
- Distributive property
- Improper form - fractions
- fraction of a fraction
- "of" means "x"
- complex fraction
- properties of division

- Visual/symbolic ✓ solution
- mult inverse/Reciprocal
- rectangular array

2. Look over the classwork you have completed and the notes you have taken. How complete is your journal including beginnings, mini-lessons, and daily math reflections? State your level of understanding and give an example as evidence of that understanding.

My journal is complete. I have taken a lot of notes on dividing fractions. I now understand how to use distributive property with multiplying fractions: If you are multiplying $6\frac{1}{4} \times \frac{2}{3}$ you would multiply $6 \times \frac{2}{3}$ and $\frac{1}{4} \times \frac{2}{3}$. Ex- $(6 \times \frac{2}{3}) + (\frac{1}{4} \times \frac{2}{3})$ then you add your answers together. Ex- $(6 \times \frac{2}{3}) + (\frac{1}{4} \times \frac{2}{3})$
$(4) + (\frac{1}{6}) = 4\frac{1}{6}$
So your product to $6\frac{1}{4} \times \frac{2}{3}$ is $4\frac{1}{6}$.

3. Look over the homework you have done. Does it include all assignments? If not, explain why. Point out parts that were challenging, difficult to understand or complete. Vocabulary entries are part of your weekly homework assignments. Look over your vocabulary for neatness and completeness. Summarize all these items.

My journal and vocabulary is complete - I have 45 words and my journal has all home work and assignments. I thought at first the distributive property was very challenging but now I understand how to do distributive proprty. ✓

4. Overall, what new understanding do you have, what questions would you like answered, and/or what help do you need?

My new understanding is about the distributive property. I understand it well because I have taven notes on it and how distributive property is used. ✓

5. Think about your effort in mathematics over the time period and your behavior and class participation. How cooperative, responsible, and supportive have you been? What improvements could you make? I am cooperative and responsible I could still work on being more supportive; and I still need to take more notes. ✓

FIGURE 7–1   *A Biweekly Self-Evaluation Submitted by Audrey*

It is important to recognize that we may learn a definiti[on]
and still not really understand it in terms of being able to [use it appro-]
priately. . . . Looking up a word in a dictionary is not, ther[efore, neces-]
sarily the best way to teach a word's meaning. (104)

My whole thesis on the value of studying mathematics thr[ough a vocabu-]
lary lens is contingent on *not* relying on dictionary definition[s until the]
concepts represented are well developed and understood. [The definitions]
in the student's personal glossary need to be constructed b[y the students.]
That's why it is so important for students to have a variety of [expressive]
venues, including self-evaluation—I keep informed, and students deepen
their understanding.

Students bump into their key math concept vocabulary at least three
times in the process of completing the biweekly self-evaluation: when they
record their responses, when the class lists their collective concepts, and
when they receive my feedback. The evaluations become a cumulative record
that flows naturally into the comprehensive trimester summative self-
evaluation.

Trimester Self-Evaluations

Students complete summative self-evaluations three times during the year.
During each trimester students engage in and complete an impressive
amount of work. As much as they grump about the self-evaluations, they
feel good about themselves when they revisit their accomplishments and
realize how much they have grown mathematically. The forms I use are
designed to help students summarize the mathematics they explored during the trimester and give evidence of their self-appraised level of accomplishment. The students also use the completed form to describe what they
have learned to their parents or guardians during the trimester portfolio
conferences.

The content and arrangement of the self-evaluation inventory changes
from trimester to trimester to match the content studied and connect it with
what comes after. The first and second trimester forms begin with a section

wing general characteristics that support mathematics achievement: work quality, process and content, and effort and classroom behavior. It is the fulfillment of a promise made the first week of school: to revisit and evaluate all areas of responsibility. I expect continuous maturation, so goals are also set for the following trimester.

Vocabulary development is central to the self-evaluation. For each unit of study, students describe concepts and big mathematical ideas accompanied by examples and illustrations. In addition, a section devoted to vocabulary asks for a certain number of words most important to the trimester's learning. Students are to select words that are not mentioned in other parts of the self-evaluation, explain them, and reinforce their explanations with examples and illustrations. Students also evaluate the quality and status of the vocabulary section (and personal word wall) in their binders.

Figure 7–2 is a completed first section of a second trimester self-evaluation form. Brief responses are provided for each of the general characteristic prompts. The principal value of this section comes from having students pause to focus on each element that contributes to a successful mathematics classroom for all of us. During portfolio conferences students select and share several responses for each of the three subsections. I want parents or guardians to understand the expectations and standards under which their children operate.

The excerpts below from trimester self-evaluations demonstrate how vocabulary and technical mathematics language are probed from two different perspectives, the unit of study and the general body of vocabulary encountered during the trimester.

Unit Perspective

In her responses to the prompts about the Moving Straight Ahead unit (see Figure 7–3), this student has used nearly a dozen technical mathematics terms, some more than once, to give convincing evidence of her comprehension of the fine points connected to linear relationships. I have

I. **General characteristics related to your mathematics achievement:**

Directions: Comment on your trimester two performance for each of the following areas.

QUALITY OF WORK PRODUCED

- Neatness/legibility
  My work is always legible and neat.

- Thoroughness
  Some of my explanations could have more.

- Accuracy with spelling and use of vocabulary
  I am always accurate with use of vocabulary and spelling.

- Labels for assignments and journal pages
  Most of my assignments and journal pages have labels.

- Attention to writing conventions
  I pay attention to writing conventions.

PROCESS AND CONTENT

- Reading and following directions
  I always read and follow directions.

- Making appropriate choices for computation
  I use my calculator too much.

- Performing computations accurately
  I almost always perform computations accurately.

- Listening and taking notes
  I listen and take notes well.

- Finding and describing patterns
  I can easily find and describe a pattern.

- Understanding concepts and explaining your thinking
  I can easily understand concepts and explain my thinking.

- Listening and contributing to class discussions
  I listen and contribute to class discussions.

- Working in a small group
  I work well in a small group.

EFFORT AND CLASSROOM BEHAVIOR

- Keeping class time focused on math
  I focus on math.

- Supporting math learning of all classmates
  I support math learning of all classmates.

- Working quietly on group as well as independent tasks
  I can work quietly on any task.

- Asking for help at appropriate times
  I ask for help when I need it.

- Using time efficiently
  I use my time efficiently.

- Making good choices when options are available
  I make good choices when options are available.

- Having seriousness of purpose
  I am serious.

- Completing and handing in assignments
  I complete and hand in all assignments.

GOALS for Trimester Three
  I would like to use my calculator less.

FIGURE 7–2   *Student Sample of a Completed "General Characteristics"*
Section in a Trimester Two Self-Evaluation Form

4. *Moving Straight Ahead* - Linear Relationships (tables, graphs, and equations)
What have you learned about linear relationships? I learned that the coefficent is also the slope. I learned how to take two coordinate points and figure out the linear equation from them. I learnal the general equation for a linear relationship. I learned some new vocabulary (e.g constant term, y-and x- intercept).

Describe how linear relationships are shown in:
tables they change at a steady rate

graphs They're are stright line

equations They fallow the general equation y=mx+b

Describe what each letter represents in the following basic equation for a linear relationship: $y = mx + b$

y is the vertical

m is the coefficent or the slope

x is the Horizontal

b is the y-intercept

Tell how you could best demonstrate what you learned and now understand about linear relationships. I would take a graph and two coordinate points then I would find the equation and make a table by just using those points.

FIGURE 7–3 *A Trimester Three Self-Evaluation Illustrating the Student's Use of Vocabulary From a Unit Perspective*

confidence in her conceptual understanding. This example illustrates how the vocabulary and concepts become one. Even so, giving students the opportunity to approach their knowledge from both avenues builds confidence while offering favorable conditions for developing ease in using technical terms.

Vocabulary Perspective

The vocabulary sections in Figures 7–4, 7–5, and 7–6 are from three different trimester self-evaluation forms. The prompts have been keyed to the activities of the specific trimester. The students whose work is shown in

Vocabulary:

Select nine words that represent your most important learning in Trimester Two. (Use entries that are different from those used in other parts of this self-evaluation.) Explain each term. Use examples or illustrations to clarify your definitions.

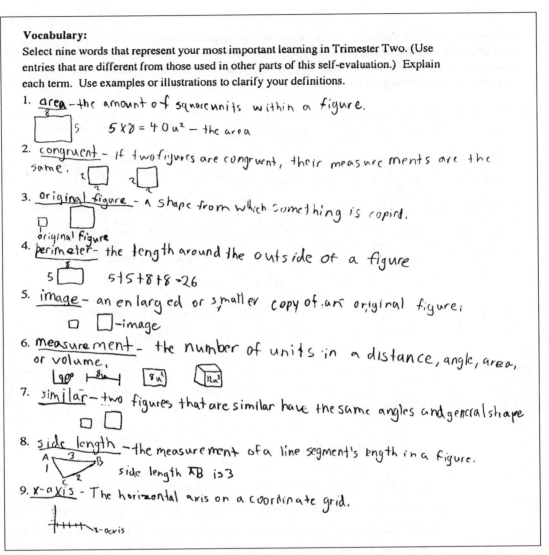

1. <u>area</u> – the amount of square units within a figure.

   □ 5   5 × 8 = 40 u² – the area

2. <u>congruent</u> – if two figures are congruent, their measurements are the same.

   □ □

3. <u>original figure</u> – a shape from which something is copied.

   □ □
   original figure

4. <u>perimeter</u> – the length around the outside of a figure

   5 □   5 + 5 + 8 + 8 = 26

5. <u>image</u> – an enlarged or smaller copy of an original figure;

   □ □ – image

6. <u>measurement</u> – the number of units in a distance, angle, area, or volume,

   90° 8u   8u²   12u³

7. <u>similar</u> – two figures that are similar have the same angles and general shape

   □ □

8. <u>side length</u> – the measurement of a line segment's length in a figure.

   A 3 B   side length AB is 3
   1   2
   C

9. <u>x-axis</u> – The horizontal axis on a coordinate grid.

   x-axis

FIGURE 7–4 *A Trimester Two Self-Evaluation Vocabulary Section Showing the Student's Use of Illustrations and Examples*

Vocabulary: What five vocabulary terms have been the most important throughout the school year? Scan your word-wall to help you decide. (Avoid any terms you listed previously.) For each term: (a) tell why it has been important and what has helped you learn, understand, and use it; and (b) give an example of how you have used it.

1. Pi: I had to revise my original understanding of it and used it to find the circumference of a circle.

2. reciprocal I was having trouble remembering this. until I got it on paper — used when multiplying

3. relationship if you understand this, you understand all of the graphing investigation (the relationship between 2 or more variables)

4. scale factor putting it in my vocab. clearified it for me. c I used it while graphing)

5. Area it was clarified when I wrote it down. I had to find it in a lot of problems

FIGURE 7–5 *A Final Self-Evaluation Vocabulary Section Showing One Student's Justifications for His Five Most Important Terms of the Year*

Figures 7–4 and 7–5 have responded seriously to the conditions set in the prompts: The first has used effective illustrated examples; the second has clearly identified the personal connection to the choice of terms as well as how the terms were used. Figure 7–6 shows a selection of terms from a broad spectrum of strands. It is fascinating how another student from

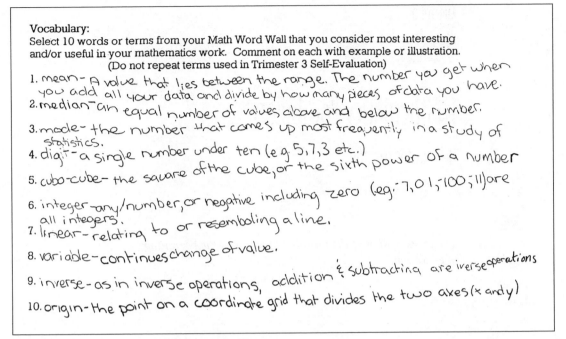

Vocabulary:
Select 10 words or terms from your Math Word Wall that you consider most interesting and/or useful in your mathematics work. Comment on each with example or illustration.
(Do not repeat terms used in Trimester 3 Self-Evaluation)

1. mean- A value that lies between the range. The number you get when you add all your data and divide by how many pieces of data you have.
2. median- an equal number of values above and below the number.
3. mode- the number that comes up most frequently in a study of statistics.
4. digit- a single number under ten (e.g 5,7,3 etc.)
5. cubo-cube- the square of the cube, or the sixth power of a number
6. integer- any/number, or negative including zero (eg; -7,0 1, 100, 11)are all integers.
7. linear- relating to or resembolling a line.
8. variable- continues change of value.
9. inverse- as in inverse operations, addition & subtracting are iverse operations
10. origin- the point on a coordinate grid that divides the two axes (x and y)

FIGURE 7–6 *A Final Self-Evaluation Vocabulary Section Showing a Selection of Terms From a Broad Spectrum of Strands*

the same group will produce a discrete selection. The variety of individual responses lets me appreciate the different gifts that students bring to learning and teaching. The value added to student performance by giving students the option to make selections within parameters is exciting to witness.

CHAPTER 8

Mathematics Vocabulary
A Focus for Writing

The investigation of the meaning of words is the beginning of education.

    —ANTISTHENES (C. 445–C. 365 B.C.)

Until now, I've been spotlighting math vocabulary as a tool used to write about mathematical concepts and ideas. This kind of writing is critical, because it affords students occasions for using their math vocabulary in a meaningful way. But the writing I'm talking about here is directed toward personal vocabulary growth. The purpose is nonsubversive and forthright—coercing students toward the mastery of useful and necessary vocabulary.

Once or twice during any given trimester or marking period, I ask my students to complete what I've come to call a "special vocabulary assignment." I connect the assignment either with a curriculum unit or a related group of useful mathematical terms that have been encountered and recorded. Whenever it occurs, this special assignment replaces the weekly vocabulary obligation.

The process begins with whole-class brainstorming while someone records the class-generated terms on chart paper. Then it is my turn to select the most significant items and give the formal assignment. Instructions are usually similar from one assignment to the next. I select between twenty and twenty-five terms and ask students to use approximately three-quarters of them in a meaningful paragraph (essay), story, letter, or poem. Whatever genre they choose, their writing must convince any reader that the author (the student doing the writing) understands and can use the vocabulary in a mathematically accurate manner.

The exercise has several characteristics that cater to the needs of middle-level students and probably other levels as well. The first characteristic is *choice*. Students are able to choose the specific terms they want to include. The parameters are clear, but there is freedom within the constraints. They are also able to choose the genre or form for their final product. If they come up with a genre I haven't anticipated, I'm happy to consider that as well. Chris always asked if he could write a song—great! The performance wasn't memorable for the mathematics, but it was memorable for its silliness. Still, Chris willingly did work that was otherwise pure torture to extract from him.

The second characteristic is the opportunity for *creativity*. Chris is an example of the student who needs the opportunity to be creative and playful with language. On the other hand, there is an equivalent invitation to be straightforward and didactic if that is the personal preference. Peggy House (1996) has published much of the work she has received as the result of similar assignments. Although she ranks the benefits of enhanced mathematical understanding as high, she feels that

> the most significant outcome of the writing activities that we have done with students has been the recognition that mathematics has a playful human dimension, a recreational fascination as well as a serious purpose, creativity as well as precision. (94)

Sometime during the winter doldrums the science teacher and I share a read-aloud with the students, a book written by Wendy Isdell (when she was an eighth grader) titled *A Gebra Named Al*. The science teacher reads for ten minutes one day, and I pick up and do ten minutes the next. The story is a cleverly developed fantasy, a dream triggered by an "impossible" *al-gebra* homework assignment. I use the book because it clearly inspires an imaginative approach to my special assignments. Students find it pretty awesome that this eighth grader has become a successful writer of mathematics and science-related fiction.

Figure 8–1 is an example of a special vocabulary assignment. Two student responses to the assignment are presented here. Nick's is a fictional "contest dialogue" (see Figure 8–2). Anne's is a free verse poem (see Figure 8–3).

There is stark contrast in the work of the two students. Nick devised an ingenious approach to cover his use of definitions already written in his binder vocabulary section, some of which show fuzzy understanding. In any case, his work should please the language arts teacher because of its consistent and appropriate use of written dialogue conventions. Anne, on the other hand, created an impressive work of poetry. Using insightful literary metaphors and relationships, she designed an imaginative environment for the related concepts and elicited a truly elegant response.

When student work from these special assignments is due, students share their work in small groups. The writing is critiqued and briefly revised

---

Special Vocabulary Assignment

Word List

addition	addends	commutative property	order	grouping
identity	subtraction	associative property	sum	subtrahend
minuend	remainder	difference	inverse	compare
zero	binary	multiplication	factors	product
multiple	array	multiplicand	multiplier	minus

Directions

Use 15 of these terms in a meaningful paragraph, story, poem, or letter to convince me of your understanding. Put a check mark next to the terms you choose and underline them in the writing.

FIGURE 8–1 *A Special Vocabulary Assignment Associated With the Study of the Four Operations*

It was time for the math bowl. My school was pitted against James Academy. Today they were going to give us a vocabulary word and we had to give a sufficient definition. The first one was for James.

"Addition," the speaker said.
"The combining of two numbers," a girl from James replied.
"Correct."
"This one's for McArthur." I was starting to get nervous.
"Addends."
"The two numbers you combine to find the sum," I said quickly.
"Correct."
"Sum."
"The answer to an addition problem."
"Correct."
"Subtraction."
"Taking away from or comparing two numbers, the inverse of addition."
"Correct."
"Subtrahend."
"The number you are taking away from the minuend," I said.
"Correct."
"Minuend."
"The number that is being compared to the subtrahend."
"Remainder."
"The number you are left with when you're taking away in subtraction or
   the number left in division when a number doesn't go in evenly."
"Correct."
"Difference."
"The answer to a subtraction when you are comparing."
"Correct."
"Binary."
"Binary means two numbers, for example addition, subtraction, division,
   and multiplication are binary operations."
"Correct."
"Multiplication."
"Repeated addition, 4×9 is $9 + 9 + 9 + 9$."
"Correct."
"Factors."
"The numbers that divide into a number evenly."

FIGURE 8–2   *Nick's Story in Response to the Special Vocabulary Assignment*

> "Correct."
> "Product."
> "The answer to a multiplication problem."
> "Correct."
> "Multiple."
> "A product of two factors."
> "Correct."
> "Multiplicand."
> "The size of the group you are multiplying."
> "Correct."
> "Last question. If McArthur's answers correctly they win."
> "Multiplier."
> "The number of groups or the number you are multiplying by."
> "Correct."
> "*I did it!*" I said triumphantly.

FIGURE 8–2   *continued.*

based on group suggestions. Group members then select one product from the group to be read aloud to the class before the homework is submitted to me for review. Anne's was among those chosen to be read aloud. This is the first of a number of mathematical poems she created throughout the year. I admit to being stunned by the level of skill and understanding apparent in Anne's writing. You'll see more of her poetry and other work later in this volume. Her work put me over the edge in thinking about sharing what I perceive as the multiple benefits of studying mathematics vocabulary. She is undeniably a major motivation for this book.

A sample of student work based on a different set of vocabulary words illustrates yet another approach to fulfilling the assignment. Ethan's exuberant Easter Bunny letter (see Figure 8–4) convinces me that his confidence with all things related to variables and coordinate graphing is appropriate.

The special vocabulary assignments clearly reinforce and deepen understanding of the concepts represented by the collection of terms, as shown in Anne and Ethan's work. This is undoubtedly an important goal, but the

The numbers line the page—
meaningless—
only numbers.
But the equations form.

Addition.
A broad definition
hiding behind the simple idea
of uniting,
combining
into something greater than either addend.
Producing an answer:
producing a sum.
The properties:
the aspects that define it—
things that prove always to be true.
Commutative.
Mix the addends.
Measure them out.
Pour them in, in any order.
The sum comes out of the oven the same.
Identity.
The magician
places the addend in his hat
and shows that there is nothing up his sleeves.
Next, he adds zero to his hat.
The room goes silent as he whispers magic words to himself . . .
and he pulls out the addend—
now the sum—
unchanged.

FIGURE 8–3   *Anne's Free Verse in Response to the Special Vocabulary Assignment*

intended purpose is to ensure many opportunities for bumping into the words of mathematics. Students encounter them in their own work as well as the work of others when they process their products in small groups and then again when they are shared orally with the class. And there's more for me as well—more opportunities to assess where my students' heads are

Subtraction.
The idea of taking away—
the minuend minus the subtrahend—
immediately suggests heartbreak in the remainder.
But truly,
it can be a difference;
something to compare the numbers with;
or, in the end, recover something lost—
an addend
from its past life in addition—
an operation echoing of its inverse—
subtraction.

The numbers line the page.
No longer meaningless
now filled with names,
with values,
with possibilities.

The equations have formed.

FIGURE 8–3 *continued.*

related to the mathematics under consideration. As I read their work, I take notes on individual issues and design previously unforeseen minilessons—the continuously exhilarating work of teaching.

Vocabulary has always been a focus of my math workshops, but one of the huge issues I had to consider on my return to the classroom was keeping balance—balance between time focused on vocabulary activities per se and time focused on mathematical content and procedures. Upon reflection, I have found that the work with vocabulary (writing, talking, word wall, and binder vocabulary section) pulls in all the other concerns and appears to do so more effectively than I could have foreseen.

Here are some excerpts from end-of-the-year student portfolio self-evaluations in response to the prompt, "What have we done in math workshop that helped you learn?"

Dear Easter Bunny,

Knowing how you are concerned with your egg production, you are probably using graphs to track it. Now just to make sure that some poor kid doesn't get left eggless your graph should have an x-axis and a y-axis, y being your dependent variable and x being your independent variable. Your independent variable should probably be the number of kids that want eggs while your dependent variable should be the number of eggs produced. Also your graph needs a scale. The scale consists of numbers that will be on the left side of your y-axis or on the bottom of the x-axis in your graph. They will show the number of pairs, which are the actual points on the graph. One number or coordinate comes up from the bottom while the other comes from the side. Where they meet, the two numbers are one coordinate pair. You plot a point on the graph where they meet. So now we've covered graphs but what about the table that should go with it. A table is the foundation for a graph. It's usually a vertical line down the middle of a horizontal line. The line separates the independent variable, which should always be on the left and the dependent variable, which should go on the right. When the numbers are across from each other they make a coordinate pair, which would make a point on the graph. Well that about wraps it up and I've got other people to annoy like Santa.

Love, Ethan

FIGURE 8–4   *Ethan's Special Vocabulary Letter to the Easter Bunny*

◆ "Writing mathematical reflections, problem-solving write-ups, vocabulary, and word wall."

◆ "I think all of the *Connected Mathematics* is helpful. I really like how it's set up, especially the mathematical reflections because they help summarize my learning."

◆ "Used writing in our math often."

◆ "Writing summaries of my math work and thinking."

◆ "The biweekly evaluations; I could step back and look at the things we covered in two weeks."

The Vocabulary Aftermath

*While vocabulary development is a product of learning,
that learning can take place in many ways, not always
as a result of teacher-directed instruction.*
—CAMILLE BLACHOWICZ AND PETER FISHER (1996, 2)

CHAPTER 9

Creating Mathematics Poetry

San Francisco's first poet laureate, Lawrence Ferlinghetti,
once asked, "What is the use of poetry these days? Isn't it
romantic illusion to think that poetry can really change
anything?"
    Poet, teacher, and anthologist Paul B. Janeczko has one
answer: "If poetry is to do more than furnish answers on a
multiple-choice test, we must relate poetry to the real world,
finding poems that are connected with something that
happened at school or in the community or in the world."
                       —MICHAEL CART (2001)

In Chapter 8 you read a poem written by Anne using addition and subtraction terminology. Anne later titled that poem "Operations Taking
Shape" and published it in the school literary magazine in a special section devoted to mathematics. Anne's poetic response to the special vocabulary assignment exemplified exciting new directions for the application of
creativity to deeper mathematical insights. Joan Countryman (1992) notes
that in a mathematics classroom where writing is normal, students become
authors of their own ideas (57). Anne is clearly the author of extraordinary
ideas that express a deep understanding of the concepts and the terms she
uses.

    Anne's remarkable work caused me to ponder the potential impact of
poetry, with its special capacity for getting attention and "making a point"
succinctly. She uses literary techniques to bring words to life, subtly attaching

relationships that deepen, clarify, and even add new meaning to quite ordinary math words. When Anne read her poem to the class, the reaction was
stunned applause. Her classmates were amazed by the amount of mathematics she added to the basic vocabulary she'd chosen.

The Teacher in Our Midst

Several months later, as the class was completing a unit on similarity, I gave
a comparable special vocabulary assignment, again based on a collection of
related terms. Once again, Anne's creative response (see Figure 9–1) was a
stunner. Her poem "Similarity" revealed complex thinking from a thirteen-
year-old student who was connecting and clarifying significant mathematical
ideas for herself and her classmates. Rheta Rubenstein, contributing to
NCTM's 1996 Yearbook, *Communication in Mathematics*, speaks of how
analogies and metaphors are particularly effective tools for helping students
assimilate technical vocabulary and understand new or challenging concepts
(217). Anne's poem illustrates this and more, using a metaphorical setting
to communicate knowledge and employ new terminology in a uniquely
cogent way. In a single page, she elucidates as well as "illustrates" with
imagery the big ideas connected to *similarity* and its properties.

This time when Anne read her poem (her group obviously chose it to
be shared), one response was, "Anne, how do you do that?" Anne immediately began describing her process—she was eager to share. I asked the
students if they would be interested in having a workshop on mathematics
poetry with Anne as the teacher and me assisting. A unanimously positive
response set Anne and me to work talking about what might be possible.

Preparation

When it comes to poetry, I am a novice. To improve my understanding I
grabbed the nearest dictionary. Typically, the etymology attracted my attention. Meanings for *poetry* that developed over time include "heap up, build,
make, arrange, and form." All the terms imply physicality—fascinating for

Similarity

The *shapes* impress themselves into the paper.
Dimensions—the basic measurements known
but little else.
The two *triangles*—proud and stunning as mountain peaks
have yet to be *compared*.

Responsibility falls to the *scale factor* to rule—
as solemnly as a judge—
whether these *shapes* have a bond,
whether they can call themselves *similar*.
The *corresponding side lengths* are looked to anxiously.
Will one increase—steadily gaining:
a crescendo of measurements?
Or will it decrease—dividing and dividing
until it's equal to the side that *corresponds* to it?
In either way there lies *similarity*.

And the *angles: corresponding*.
They must also be measured out
to make the recipes *similar*—
they must measure the same.

But the *scale factor* has not shared all—
like a flowering plant there is still one more bud to be pushed open,
to bloom.
The *area*.
The *scale factor* looks into the magic mirror—
sees itself multiplied . . .
squared . . .
scale factor times *scale factor*.
And we uncover the buried treasure:
The number of times the area is multiplied
to reach the size of its *image*.

FIGURE 9–1 *Anne's Free Verse Poem Submitted for the Special Vocabulary Assignment Connected to the Study of Similarity*

> But wait . . .
> listen . . .
> the *triangle* has one more secret
> that dwells below the surface.
> It also *rep-tiles*.
> When the *triangles* that are *congruent* to it—
> a smattering of clones that fall from the sky like snowflakes—
> are pieced together in a complicated jigsaw puzzle of geometry,
> they form a larger *similar shape*.
> The *transformation* is complete.
>
> These tall proud *polygons* now have meanings beyond *dimensions*.
> There are words—sure things that define them,
> that *compare* them.
> They are part of the complicated world of mathematics.
>
> —*Anne Atwell-McLeod*

FIGURE 9–1 *continued.*

a word that has come to represent a form and style of concentrated, imaginative, powerful composition. It is a form that most always demands elegance, more instructive even than Einstein's ultimately elegant equation for the Theory of Relativity.

I also looked to author and poet Mary Oliver for help in understanding the genre and its processes. In *Blue Pastures* (1995) she writes about the changes taking place as to the acceptable subjects of poetry:

> Unlocked forever were the gates outside which the uninvited subjects of poems were tossing their pretty heads, and not-so-pretty heads. We no longer talk about what subject matter is appropriate and what is not so appropriate. It is all appropriate. (103)

Oliver helped me further understand Anne's way of thinking and her special affinity for poetry:

> The poem exists—indeed, gets itself written—in the relation between the man [Anne] and the world. The three ingredients of poetry: the mystery of the universe [unfolding patterns of mathematics], spiritual

curiosity [belief in the relationships that emerged in Anne's mind], the energy of language [Anne's poem]. (57)

Poetry, after all, is not a miracle. It is an effort to formalize (ritualize) individual moments and the transcending effects of these moments into a music that all can use. It is the song of our species. (59)

I was now fascinated with the genre and how it could enhance mathematics vocabulary and learning. Poetry has power; mathematics has power. They share an approachable yet ethereal elegance, at once concrete and abstract. I consulted Nancie, the language arts teacher. She shared my excitement about the potential benefits of combining mathematics and poetry. She offered support and helpful suggestions for genres that would be appropriate for the expected challenge—she *knew* these kids, especially their experience with poetry. Armed with Nancie's "Options for a Group Response to a Poem" (Atwell 1998, 426), a list of rules for haiku, and the format for a tritina, Anne and I met to plan the "poetry and mathematics" workshop.

Lesson Planning

The plan came together with an outline of the sequence of events for the workshop. In the meantime the class had moved on to the study of integers, and Anne wrote yet another awesome poem. Anne and I knew right away that she had to read that poem, "Number Line" (see Figure 9–2), aloud to begin the workshop. The rest of the class, myself included, would follow along, each with our own copy. We would look for and mark three elements from Nancie's "Options for a Group Response to a Poem." The options Anne selected were:

- ◆ Underline your favorite lines.
- ◆ Mark the metaphors.
- ◆ Mark the lines in the poem most important to the mathematics.

Once the poem had been read, the class and I would share the things we had highlighted and compare them with what Anne's choices might be.

Number Line

Integers.
The broad term evelops
the *negative* and *postive* alike.
It accepts the simplicity of their wholeness,
not bothering to include the more basic of the *decimals*
whom it leaves to the less exclusive title
of *rational* numbers.
(Reading between the lines is too hard.
The endlessly complex parts and scraps
clutter the neatly kept integers).
And *zero.*
The number that can be interpreted
as something so complicated
(silence stretching on forever
in an empty room)
or seen as simply nothing
(a mind goes blank).
It's surrounded by *positive* to the right,
negative to the left,
but shielded from being either.
Lost in the black hole
of its own ominous O.

Absolute values transcend the *integers.*
They see beyond *negative* and *positive*
to the number's true core.
They are brutal and decisive.
Knowing just exactly what a number is all about,
reflecting its position in the world.

Opposites string together both worlds
by giving each integer a glimpse
of what lies beyond *zero.*
(A mirror throws back a distorted reflection.)
(Black becomes white
as the thin layer of film
is held up to the light.)

FIGURE 9–2   *Anne's Free Verse Poem Submitted for the Special Vocabulary Assignment Connected to the Study of Integers*

Looking beyond *integers,*
rationals,
the unreasonable must be dealt with—
π, $\sqrt{2}$—
irrational numbers
that will outlive us all
as they race towards a finish line
that will never come.
The other, more dignified numbers make guesses,
approximations
(even they don't know
where these numbers will turn next).

The numbers manage, though,
to band together.
They take comfort in their own consistencies,
their never faltering definitions.
They are what's *real,*
these groups of numbers.
They are what's concrete—
what will be here in the future,
what has been there all along.

—Anne Atwell-McLeod

FIGURE 9–2   *continued.*

At this point I would ask Anne to describe how she goes about planning
for a math poem, referring specifically to the three poems of hers with which
the class would now be familiar.

As Anne shared her strategies with me in our planning meeting, she
decided that it would be good for me to create a poem similar to the ones
the class would be asked to write. Once I had the experience, during the
workshop I could share my struggles with the class, along with my very first
attempt to create a math poem. I agreed to try.

The students were to select three terms from their mathematics vocabulary and write a poem in either of two formats—tritina or haiku. The demands of the two formats offer good contrasting options: The haiku is brief,

fun, and can be uncomplicated, while the tritina is complex and demand-
ing, requiring more brainwork and word gnashing. Here are the specifics:

Haiku: Three lines
         Line one—five syllables
         Line two—seven syllables
         Line three—five syllables

Tritina: Select three words.
           Create three stanzas and an envoy according to the follow-
           ing constraints:
           I.   Line one ends in word one
                Line two ends in word two
                Line three ends in word three
           II. Line one ends in word three
                Line two ends in word one
                Line three ends in word two
           III. Line one ends in word two
                Line two ends in word three
                Line three ends in word one

ENVOY.   One line using all three words

My experience writing the poem was just what Anne had said—essential to the workshop. Only by role-playing a realistically assigned writing
experience could I effectively ask students to use the format in a mathematical context and respond to their questions or support them through the process. We both decided I needed to tackle a tritina, which I had never heard
of before. (In contrast, many students had created tritinas in writing class.)

I did eventually tease out "A Triangular Tritina" (see Figure 9–3). It was
a stressful experience. It was unknown territory, it was risky, and I sensed
there was a lot at stake. Mary Oliver wrote, "It takes about seventy hours
to drag a poem into the light" (59). I didn't count the hours, but seventy
hours seemed no exaggeration. The poem became a family project. I emailed
my son, who has a flair for writing, for moral support. Over a period of

> ### A Triangular Tritina
>
> Three dimensions—count them—one of the bold polyhedra.
> Faces drawn together forming a prism,
> Marching in closed formation, three regal rectangles.
>
> They're everywhere—doors, windows, walls, ceilings—the pervasive
> rectangles.
> Forming a plethora of polyhedra.
> Parallel and congruent, crown and dais—aha! It is a prism.
>
> Five faces—count them—distinguished among all others, a triangular
> prism.
> Parallel edges—three sets, parallel faces—one pair, held fast by tall stately
> rectangles,
> Emerging royally among the polyhedra.
>
> Stability crowns her "Queen of Polyhedra"—with three tall rectangles,
> this regal prism owns the rainbow.

FIGURE 9–3   *The Teacher's Tritina, Created as Part of the Lesson Preparation for Writing Mathematics Poetry*

several days I used Anne's suggestions: listed, wrote, crossed out, rewrote, and asked several of my students to have a writing conference with me. That really helped, and the poem finally came together. My son ended up offering more than moral support. He replied with a couple of haikus (see Figure 9–4) I could use with the class. We were ready to go ahead with the lesson.

I checked carefully against the criteria for a tritina to be sure I had all elements—it is what I would expect of my students! Every time I looked at the "poem" I tweaked the language a bit more, teasing out more mathematics

> ### Walking Your Hypotenuse
>
> A hypotenuse
> is the shortest way to go
> back to where you were.
>
> ### A Little Math Primer
>
> Two plus two is four,
> four times two is even more, but
> power of four rules!

FIGURE 9–4   *Two Haikus Created by My Son, Matthew Murray, as Part of the Lesson Preparation for Writing Mathematics Poetry*

and playing with the words, but enough now! Armed with these products we proceeded with the workshop.

After Anne read her poem and the class and I responded with our favorite lines, talked about the metaphors, and determined the lines most important to the mathematics, Anne described how she goes about developing a poem:

> Because I'm starting with a list of words, I start by thinking about all of the words and what they mean in broad terms—more than their literal definitions. It's all about connections between words, their mathematical connections as well as their connections to real life. Then I select individual terms and begin to search for metaphors. What is it similar to outside of mathematics? I start with one expansion on what it could be, usually something crazy, and see where it goes. If the connection doesn't develop for me right away, that's okay because I can try something else crazy. It's a fun process. With the similarity list, as I thought about a triangle, a mountain seemed like an interesting real-life triangle and it carried me along to other connected vocabulary terms that were important to similarity. I look deliberately for connections between the words and that leads me to the form of the poem.

Then she asked me to talk about my experience as a beginner and read my poem. As is the custom, I gave copies of my work to the students. They were unusually interested in having their math teacher operate in "foreign territory" and appreciated my son's contributions as well. They analyzed my product using the options Anne had suggested and delighted in commenting upon their teacher's work.

Class members offered their own personal ideas about developing a poem and then we talked about the assignment. They understood they were each to select three mathematics terms from their vocabulary lists and develop either a tritina or three haikus. The assignment was in lieu of their regular weekly vocabulary assignment. They were to use the mathematical terms in a meaningful way and convince me of their conceptual understanding. The students were encouraged to help one another, but they were each responsible for a final product of their own. There was time to ask clarifying questions and begin the process in class. Then it became a homework assignment due in one week. I had learned for myself, and described for them, the time and energy that it took for me to feel successful.

Results

I gained insights about my students through their responses to the assignment. In some instances it was appreciation for their skill with the genre, in others it was their feelings and attitudes, and in still others, their sense of humor as well as the mathematics they chose.

Marcia selected *similarity*. Her tritina (see Figure 9–5) captured key ideas as well as the special case for congruent figures. I have to believe she was thinking seriously about geometry and relationships as she crafted her poem, more seriously than if she had been using a more direct manner of telling about figures, images, and being similar.

Brooks struggled throughout the year to write about his thinking in mathematics. He found the haiku format friendly. Although he took poetic license with syllable counts, he gave his impression of a concept he found fascinating (see Figure 9–6).

Similar Figures and Images
Congruent figures—
two shapes exactly the same—similar
mirror images.

Original image—
enlarged into a different figure
identical shape, different size, but similar.

Similarity—
two related images
with almost matching figures.

Congruent figures can be images, but they are similar.

—*Marcia Conley Carter*

FIGURE 9–5   *Marcia's Tritina on Similarity*

Absolute Value
A number ignoring
All signs and symbols. That's
Absolute value.

—*Brooks Kerr*

FIGURE 9–6 *Brooks' Haiku on Absolute Value*

Nick delighted in an opportunity to express subtle and not-so-subtle relationships of more advanced mathematical terms to their counterparts in real life. This revealed to me a broader and deeper involvement with the world of mathematics than I had encountered in class. I grinned all over as I read and reread his "take on mathematics" (see Figure 9–7). Nick finds homonyms a resource for puns and fun.

Alexis used haiku to express her understanding of *irrational numbers*. The images conjured up through her amazing choice of metaphors added to my own understanding of the term. A brief poem of this quality (see Figure 9–8)

My Take on Mathematics
The ratio of the circumference of a circle to its diameter is pi.
The study of random events is chaos.
A group of numbers aligned in a box is a matrix.

The popular science fiction film starring Keanu Reeves is *The Matrix*.
Rhubarb, apple, and pecan are of another variety of "pi."
Extreme confusion and disorder are a less chaotic chaos.

Randomness, and humanity's sultry confusion are chaos.
A matrix can relate to another matrix.
Irrational but very useful is pi.

Mathematics is a matrix of chaos (and should be rewarded with pi).

—*Nick Miller*

FIGURE 9–7 *Nick's "Take on Mathematics" in Tritina Format*

> **Irrational Number**
> A sprawling wasteland,
> A digit cacophony,
> Lacking rhythm.
> —*Alexis Kellner Becker*

FIGURE 9–8 *Alexis' Elegant Haiku Description of an Irrational Number*

is the epitome of elegance and cause for celebration. It tells me volumes about Alexis and her otherwise hidden potential.

And then there's Forrest, with his need to stray slightly outside the boundaries. The assignment was too definitive and too "mathy" for him. His carefully crafted tritina (see Figure 9–9) communicates mixed feelings about mathematics—all with good humor—even though he hasn't clearly defined three math terms within its walls.

> **The Spiderweb of Mathematics**
> A spiderweb resembles mathematics
> The spider resembles numbers
> The trapped helpless fly resembles me.
>
> And along comes the spider to engulf me.
> I am one of the countless victims of mathematics,
> And the annoying building blocks of mathematics, numbers.
>
> But Miki has developed an immunity to the cruel numbers,
> And has even grown to liking mathematics,
> With [more resistance] to the sticky spiderweb, she rescues the
>   unfortunate captive: ME!
>
> So now I steer clear of mathematics and it's devilish counterpart,
>   numbers, but just in case, I have Miki there to help me.
> —*Forrest Carver*

FIGURE 9–9 *Forrest's Feelings About Mathematics in Tritina Format*

I was pleased to have the students respond with such variety to the math poetry workshop and assignment. They opened to the opportunity, had fun, and stretched the mathematics and language connection. For her completion of the class assignment Anne took great pleasure in writing the mathematics tritina in Figure 9–10, elegantly describing the process of working with data.

The experience led me to ruminate more about the teaching of mathematics. How much straying from official curriculum demands can be justified? What level of value does math poetry hold for all students? The poetry workshop offered variety, which middle-level students thrive on, and for the majority there was evidence of thinking about, and solving problems with, important mathematical ideas. Poet Paul Engle revealed a unique mathematical connection when he commented: "Poetry is ordinary language raised to the Nth power" (Simpson 1988, 319). Now, I don't think I could teach mathematics without incorporating the reading and writing of related poetry.

Howard Gardner established his theory of multiple intelligences in 1983 with the publication of *Frames of Mind*. It was targeted to psychologists but

---

Tritina

Before analysis, the data
is only numbers;
bereft of representation in table or line plot,

until the plot
thickens. Given order, this data
and its numbers

range. The former chaos of these numbers
dies down—they're saved from the storm, and the only step left: to plot
the points and trace the story told by the data.

(Plot the numbers in pairs and send them off into the ark. The data has
      been here.)

—Anne Atwell-McLeod

FIGURE 9–10 *Anne's Tritina Summary of Working With Data*

has proven critical to important changes in education. Following are thought-provoking comments he made in an interview (Brandt 1993) with Ron Brandt, the executive editor of the Association for Supervision and Curriculum Development:

> When you've encountered an idea in your own way and brought your own thinking to bear, the idea becomes much more a part of you. . . .
>
> It's important to provide what I call "multiple entry points." Kids don't all learn the same way; they don't all find the same things interesting. In fact, based on my theory of multiple intelligences introduced in *Frames of Mind,* I'd say that you can approach almost any rich topic in a whole variety of ways.
>
> We need to give kids a chance in school to enter the room by different windows, so to speak—but be able to see the relationships among the different types of windows.

Gardner's comment adds another dimension to windows, doors, and secret passageways. In the future, I expect to learn more about the impact of a poetry–mathematics connection. For now, it offers another option for using vocabulary to learn mathematics, and for some students it is a uniquely effective and engaging window.

CHAPTER 10

Putting Vocabulary Learning Strategies Into Context

It makes sense to look on "knowing" a word as a continuous process that can be affected by meaningful encounters with words and by instruction aimed at helping learners develop a network of understanding.
—CAMILLE BLACHOWICZ AND PETER FISHER (1996, 5)

I wrote this book, and gathered the student work showcased in it, because I wanted to demonstrate that cultivating a strong mathematics vocabulary matters. First, it matters for me personally: Learning the vocabulary opened doors to conversations that made mathematics a more human endeavor for me. It also matters for me as a teacher of mathematics: I understand mathematical relationships and concepts more deeply when I connect the signs, symbols, and words that describe them and use those connections to communicate more clearly with my students. Finally and most important, it matters for the mathematical success of my students: Understanding and using mathematics vocabulary to justify and describe their problem-solving exposes them to a deeper understanding of concepts as well as the important relationships between them. Educational researchers who have delved into the subtleties of the relationship between vocabulary acumen and general academic success (see Allen 1999 and Blachowicz and Fisher 1996) have contributed significantly to the current understanding of word power. I'm grateful to them.

All the strategies I talk about in this book contribute to an overall study of vocabulary. Studying vocabulary is *not* looking up a list of terms in a dictionary at the beginning of a unit or consulting the glossary at the end of the textbook. It is a developmental process that honors the individual characteristics and needs of students. I have previously cited Camille Blachowicz and Peter Fisher for their study of vocabulary research and their resulting suggestions for developing a strong vocabulary program in any content area. Let me repeat their suggestions:

1. Immerse students in words.
2. Encourage students to be active in making connections between words and experiences.
3. Encourage students to personalize word learning.
4. Build on multiple sources of information.
5. Help students to control their learning.
6. Aid students in developing independent strategies.
7. Assist students in using words in meaningful ways; meaningful use leads to long-lasting learning. (7)

In order to analyze the contribution of each element of my vocabulary program and show how it relates to these seven research-supported guidelines, I have organized all the activities from Chapters 1 through 9 into five categories:

1. classroom management
2. classroom culture
3. classroom rituals
4. assessment and evaluation
5. specific vocabulary activities

This range of categories demonstrates how the activities permeate the mathematics program, providing support for vocabulary growth from various perspectives. These categories, each with its list of activities, are the result of the conscious implementation of a program that immerses students in mathematics vocabulary, surrounding them with the essential sounds, symbols, and words they will need for effective mathematics communication.

Connecting the individual means for building an effective mathematics vocabulary to a larger overarching structure makes it easier to create a vocabulary program suited to the needs of your students.

Classroom Management Activities

Classroom management encompasses ways of administering and conducting the business of the classroom (solving problems, exploring patterns, and generally gaining knowledge) in order to accomplish the curricular goals. I designed, organized, and implemented a number of management techniques to support a strong vocabulary web throughout the mathematics curriculum:

- ◆ Maintain journal as a section of the three-ring binder.
- ◆ Work with a partner.
- ◆ Problem-solve, explore, and prepare presentations with small groups of three or four.
- ◆ Develop rubrics and rules for listening, contributing, and writing collaboratively.
- ◆ Develop a personal cumulative mathematics vocabulary using the word wall index.
- ◆ Establish and follow structure for writing about problem solving.
- ◆ Inform parents.
- ◆ Keep individual homework logs.
- ◆ Work with language arts teacher as appropriate.

The activities in this category are particularly effective in actively involving students, personalizing word learning, using multiple sources of information, providing multiple opportunities for vocabulary use, and encouraging long-term conceptual understanding (Blachowicz and Fisher suggestions 2, 3, 4, 6, and 7).

Classroom Culture Activities

Classroom culture encompasses customs and ways of interacting and behaving within the classroom. The mathematics culture is established during the first days and weeks of the school year. All members of the group are expected to understand and share responsibility for maintaining the following accepted practices:

- ◆ Establish expectations and guidelines for all aspects of classroom interaction and student responsibility.
- ◆ Model using language, giving evidence, and explaining thinking.
- ◆ Focus mathematics discourse on students:
  - ◆ Address math comments to one another, not the teacher.
  - ◆ Address questions to one another, not the teacher.
- ◆ Use problems, questions, current media, and professional literature to stimulate discourse.
- ◆ Listen for and note use of mathematics vocabulary.
- ◆ Write daily for various purposes, especially describing thinking and reasoning.
- ◆ Define terms in language students are currently comfortable with (not dictionary definitions) using examples and illustrations.
- ◆ Acknowledge current level of related vocabulary knowledge to begin each unit.
- ◆ Use a variety of resources and references to verify, refine, and extend ideas.

The strongest connections for these classroom culture strategies are to the Blachowicz and Fisher suggestions 1 and 2: Immerse students in mathematics language while actively connecting technical language to mathematics experiences. They also offer broad support for the other program suggestions.

Classroom Rituals

Classroom rituals are activities or procedures that happen at regular intervals—daily, weekly, biweekly, monthly, or every trimester. They are the foundation for ensuring subtle but frequent vocabulary practice. They include:

◆ Practice listening skills with paraphrasing and note taking.

◆ Brainstorm new vocabulary weekly, keeping a record on classroom chart paper.

◆ Survey class weekly for vocabulary and individually developed definitions.

◆ Practice vocabulary with vocabulary game warm-ups.

◆ Enter five vocabulary words weekly into personal vocabulary and word wall.

◆ Record daily reflections in journal.

◆ Process homework daily in small groups.

◆ Complete biweekly self-evaluations.

◆ Survey class for concepts on biweekly self-evaluation before submission.

◆ Process writing assignments with peer evaluations, feedback, and revisions.

◆ Share problem solutions and creative mathematics products.

The strengths of the rituals are immersion, personalizing word learning, giving students control of their learning, developing independence, and providing multiple opportunities for meaningful use. (See Blachowicz and Fisher suggestions 1, 3, 5, and 6.)

Assessment and Evaluation Activities

Assessment and evaluation activities share the following characteristics: An inventory of completed work and current knowledge is prepared; a value for the inventory is determined; and new goals or a new direction is established.

- ◆ Complete math survey (in September and June).
- ◆ Use the assessment cycle (gather evidence, interpret, reflect, and advance knowledge) as the basis for describing solution strategies, whether in homework, journals, problem-solving write-ups, or mathematical reflections.
- ◆ Complete biweekly self-evaluations. (Formative)
- ◆ Summarize learning by writing a mathematical reflection for each investigation.
- ◆ Complete trimester self-evaluations. (Summative)
- ◆ Submit vocabulary list for monthly evaluation and feedback.
- ◆ Submit journal for monthly evaluation and feedback.

The strongest contributions that assessment and evaluation activities make to the comprehensive vocabulary program are in helping students make word–experience connections, giving them opportunities to use vocabulary meaningfully, and helping them develop long-term conceptual understanding with continuously more sophisticated language (Blachowicz and Fisher suggestions 2, 6, and 7).

Specific Vocabulary Activities

Specific vocabulary activities build vocabulary directly. They grow out of the activities in the other categories, which maintain, reinforce, and give the contextual fuel that keeps the vocabulary learning machine working.

- ◆ Prepare and perform poems from *Math Talk: Mathematical Ideas in Poems for Two Voices* (by Theoni Pappas) with partner.
- ◆ Respond to math focus articles from current media.

- Deal with vocabulary demons—etymological connections, interdisciplinary connections, alliterative mnemonic techniques, and practice.
- Facilitate student–teacher collaborative lessons.
- Create vocabulary games.
- Create unit-based vocabulary concept maps to use for portfolio presentation.
- Complete and process special vocabulary assignments.
- Write mathematics poetry.

This final category hits the jackpot for its significant contribution to each of the suggested elements for a vital vocabulary development program. These activities, emerging out of current need and context, help build mathematics students who are fluent in the language of mathematics.

The Results Are In

Each of Blachowicz and Fisher's program suggestions is strongly implemented by at least two categories of activities. Subtly and sometimes subversively, all of the program suggestions are supported by each of the categories. The benefits of cultivating a strong mathematics vocabulary in mathematics classrooms are great.

Epilogue

*So what sticks? What kind of learning lasts beyond a
given year that we can grab hold of to guide our vision? I
contend that what stays with us from our education are
patterns: patterns of behavior, patterns of thinking,
patterns of interaction. These patterns make up . . .
intellectual character. Through [these patterns] we show
what we are made of as thinkers and learners.*

— RON RITCHHART (2002, 9)

everal years ago my granddaughter Kendra visited Bowdoin College,
her first foray into postsecondary possibilities and adventures. An en-
thusiastic young woman who had just completed her freshman year at
Bowdoin escorted Kendra's tour group throughout the campus. At the conclusion of the tour, they assembled with similar groups for discussion and
an opportunity to ask questions. The father of a prospective student asked,
"As a freshman at Bowdoin College what was your biggest surprise?" The
young lady's response, without hesitation, was, "My biggest surprise was
the amount of writing required in mathematics class—I was totally un-
prepared for that!" Knowing my passion for teaching mathematics in meaningful ways, Kendra couldn't wait to share this with me.

I was grateful for the anecdote. First, it was evidence that others in the
business of mathematics education (even a Bowdoin College mathematics

professor) understood and practiced using language strategies to support student learning in mathematics. Second, the incident nudged me to think about how a vocabulary-infused math experience might affect future mathematical or general educational endeavors. Are there long-range positive benefits for students that can be documented?

It wasn't long before I came across a close-to-home case in point. The writing teacher brought me the following final eighth-grade essay:

Connecting: Math and Writing

Why do Dead Monkeys Smell Bad? This mnemonic, telling me to divide, multiply, subtract, and bring down, meant nothing to me as I muttered it to myself while contemplating a long-division problem. I only became more confused. What I wanted to know lay beyond memorized procedures and one-word answers.

I'm a word person. Numbers don't mean anything to me unless there are words behind them—reasons I can verbalize. Unfortunately, I didn't know this for most of my school career. Simple things like borrowing when subtracting puzzled me. I didn't understand how it worked or where those borrowed numbers came from that made subtraction possible. Because I didn't understand, I always thought I was bad at math.

In seventh grade I moved into a new math class with a new math teacher. Here, the approach was different. We solved problems not only by finding the answer, but also by writing about why we thought it was the answer and describing the work we'd done to arrive at the solution: Not only how to borrow when subtracting, but just what it meant to move those borrowed numbers around.

I learned how to write up problems: How to describe my solutions and create my own general rules based on the evidence I'd gathered while solving problems. This became as satisfying to me as having the perfect ending to a story in writing class.

Sometimes I was asked to write poems using mathematics vocabulary we'd been studying. This was an incredible opportunity for me— to combine the best of both worlds and learn more deeply about math by bringing my imagination to bear on the ideas of mathematics.

It also helped when my teacher asked me to record and reflect on what we'd done in class each day in a math journal. Thinking about the bigger ideas and concepts behind the math work of a given day helps me to connect related work in my mind.

Writing has always helped me as a way of understanding the world. Writing and generalizing in math made me understand not only how and why strategies and principles worked for a particular problem, but how and why they might work for other similar problems. Viewing math this way, as a process that makes sense because of its connections, rather than something completely arbitrary and spontaneous, made it less overwhelming—a subject that, complicated as it was, could be mastered.

Through writing about my thinking, through analyzing the process, I clarified math for myself. It finally stuck. Now I love the science of mathematics.

—Anne Atwell-McLeod

The idea that an emphasis on vocabulary and other language connections could impact a student's motivational pathway to learning mathematics had not yet surfaced in my thinking. And here was Anne, articulating exactly that. Anne's essay revealed how specific cultural elements of the vocabulary-infused mathematics classroom affected her.

Ron Ritchhart (2002), of the Harvard Graduate School of Education, describes the "cultural forces," determined through his research, that give a classroom its framework for functioning as a learning community. They are:

1. Expectations for student thinking and learning that the teacher conveys.

2. Routines and structures that the teacher employs to guide the life of the classroom.

3. Language that the teacher and students use and the kinds of conversations in which they engage.

4. Learning opportunities, work, or activities the teacher creates for students.

5. How the teacher behaves and what the teacher models for students.

6. The attitudes the teacher and students convey about learning.

7. The interactions and relationships between the teacher and students as well as among the students themselves.

8. The physical environment and artifacts present in the room. (146–47)

In her essay, Anne identifies several of these forces as key to her transformation: her teacher's expectations, the routines and structures that supported the curriculum, the focus on the language of mathematics, the teacher's attitude toward learning mathematics, and the learning opportunities afforded her. In addition, she clearly values the interactions and relationships between teacher and students.

Ritchhart's characteristics are confirming checkpoints for me, a topological map of classroom culture benchmarks. Any teacher contemplating the potential value of changing practice or reflecting on problematic elements of his or her classroom will find the list a useful guide. Each cultural force represents an opportunity for classroom self-assessment—an audit of current classroom conditions. The framework allows the vocabulary enhancement techniques set forth in the previous ten chapters to be evaluated. What potential value does each strategy add to a mathematics classroom's learning community? How might a specific vocabulary strategy flesh out your ideal classroom culture *and* support the learning of mathematics?

For example, one of my expectations (Ritchhart's first benchmark) is that every student contribute to the learning community on a regular basis. Therefore, I institute routine ways that coerce opportunity and develop necessary skills. One such routine occurs every Friday during the class "sweep" when each student shares a current vocabulary entry with its definition—no repetitions until the possibilities are exhausted. It becomes part of how we do business: each student knows the regular opportunities for contributing. No one can hide. Phaelon, now a high school junior, describes that experience as a high point. This is her response for her most important recollection of seventh- and eighth-grade math classes: "Going around the circle and getting a chance to put a vocabulary word I'd chosen on the chart and getting the chance to explain it."

Exploring Student Reactions

In my continued effort to look for evidence of long-range impacts for student learning, I recently enjoyed Saturday brunch with eight former students. (I was stunned by how sleepy these ordinarily frisky teenagers appeared at 11 A.M. on a Saturday morning!) The students are sophomores, juniors, and seniors at six different area high schools. We chatted about their recollections of seventh- and eighth-grade mathematics. Their willingness to gather with me during precious weekend time indicated they had positive memories of their experiences.

They spoke first of the vocabulary lists and the word-wall folder and how challenging it was to keep the collection current. Five words each week was heavy duty—until we started the brainstorming ritual of listing all the words the class had bumped into during that week. (I began doing this for two reasons: because I heard students say they couldn't find five new terms, and students had used terms unrelated to what we were doing or had completed.) The task then became doable and routine; there were more than enough word candidates to satisfy several weeks' worth of word entries. Teachers, make note: The student "voice of experience" is saying that vocabulary brainstorming is an *essential* part of acquiring a substantial personal mathematics vocabulary.

Their memory of paraphrasing practice triggered an interesting dialogue. Ethan brought up paraphrasing as a favorite activity as well as "the best" vocabulary practice for him. Emily remembered it differently: "Ethan, that was just listening skill practice." The brief discussion that followed convinced us all that paraphrasing developed both vocabulary and listening skills. Ethan concluded by remembering the guideline of using a term at least twenty-seven times in order to make it an automatic part of his repertoire. I was amazed that he remembered our long-ago initial classroom conversation about the challenge of mastering the language of mathematics—finding opportunities to use mathematics terms in meaningful ways close to thirty times each. My comment about the research on vocabulary acquisition obviously impressed him. Ethan and Emily are currently seniors looking forward to college careers in engineering and "maybe mathematics, French, education," respectively.

Alexis gave the most impassioned contribution to our lunch conversation. She talked in earnest about her belief as she entered seventh grade that math was an entirely separate element of life that she simply had to endure. She didn't think "that way" and math (arithmetic really) didn't make sense to her, but she would do her best. Like Anne, the experience of using words as a way to talk about the mathematics was a defining moment for Alexis. Being asked to describe her thinking simply "knocked her socks off." Discovering and describing relationships along with explaining her own way of solving interesting problems totally engrossed her in the mathematics–logic–language connection. She fondly recalled reading Theoni Pappas' books in the eighth grade as an optional activity and discovering and explaining the fallacy in the proof of "one equals two." Alexis has since taken two philosophy courses, being amazed by and drawn to the "remarkable" similarity to mathematical reasoning. Although Alexis is truly a mathematician with a strong linguistic sense, loving the precision required for logical presentation, she avoids math courses because the way they are taught generally makes no sense to her. Alexis is currently a junior, interested in drama, community service, thinking, and metacognition.

As the conversation moved along, all of the students talked extensively about how problem-solving write-ups and special vocabulary assignments provided a firm foundation for the demands of high school and whatever should come next. Tyler was especially articulate recalling how *describing his understanding actually created the understanding.* He considered the writing an important training tool that developed his skill in describing his thinking succinctly to others. He said he feels he is especially effective in this regard, and I concur. Problem-solving write-ups were for him the essential confidence builder. All of the students echoed his sentiments, and several mentioned the stories and poems they created using mathematics vocabulary.

Ceysa recalled the "I Have, Who Has?" vocabulary warm-ups as a favorite activity that she has since learned to adapt for class projects. Anne brought up how the MATHCOUNTS problems helped her learn to think outside the box and provided yet more opportunities to use technical vocabulary to describe her unique approach to solving a problem. Others agreed.

Emily related how her freshman math teacher appreciated her many questions. The teacher watched carefully for student reactions and understanding, urging them to question elements they were unsure of. However, all her math teachers after that told her and her parents that "Emily has no patience—she asks questions continually." But Emily said she will continue to question because "I really want to know and understand." Good for her!

The last significant topic of conversation centered on their current mathematics classes. In response to a particular issue that was raised, I suggested they bring the issue up in their current math classes. Emily dramatically exclaimed, "Miki, our math classes do *not* have a discussion format!" Everyone resoundingly echoed her statement. So I asked them to describe their mathematics classes for me, a description I have summarized below:

1. Begin class by going over the homework.
2. A fifteen- to twenty-minute lesson (longer for an eighty-minute class).
3. Work on the new homework assignment for the remainder of the period.

I can't begin to express my deep and sincere concern and disappointment. I joined with others in the mathematics education community and put enormous effort and resources into the improvement of mathematics experiences for all school children over the past fifteen years. Since these students attended six different high schools within a fifty-mile radius, it was obvious there is still a great deal of work to do. I was devastated and depressed, revived only by the strength of this stalwart group of young people who had sacrificed a Saturday afternoon to share their thoughts with me. I am confident that they know how to learn mathematics and that they are clearly in charge of that learning.

Other former students unable to attend the Saturday gathering offered their feedback through the mail. I am including key elements from their comments.

To support understanding and long-lasting learning several students recommend that teachers use more than one strategy to teach a lesson, and have students write about math, use vocabulary in stories, do problem-solving write-ups, and reflect daily. These students find it easier to remember the mathematics when they write about it. They also find the math much easier to learn when they understand why and how it works.

Nick and Ruthie attribute strong vocabulary and problem-solving skills to their junior high experience recalling that math write-ups forced them to understand and to communicate their processes clearly. The vocabulary helped them learn more easily in high school, study math efficiently, and communicate with correct mathematical terms.

Writing stories made it easier to understand the vocabulary, and reflections were a good way to review concepts. Audrey notices that she's the only one in her current geometry class who understands the vocabulary and the procedures because of her earlier work. She's aware that she has more basic knowledge than the other students do. For Colby, he finds the knowledge of vocabulary itself useful when trying to explain his problems to teachers and that writing it out always works in his favor.

And finally, high school junior Brenna confirms reaching one of my primary goals. She is aware that she understands concepts deeper but not always in the same terms. For example, when something new is explained she frequently recognizes connections to an underlying concept understanding from seventh and eighth grade. On that positive note I'll conclude.

Designing for Now and the Future

The fabric of a learner-centered mathematics classroom environment is woven using the basic structures of mathematics content and its processes. The content and processes provide the fundamental "woof and warp," but the texture of the classroom, its "intellectual character" (Ritchhart 2002), depends on the embellishments—the routines, rituals, strategies, expectations, and other cultural details designed or selected and instituted by the teacher. The embellishments I've shared here were conceived and developed through a vocabulary-building lens. This word approach is not magic for all students, but the evidence from my experience is that it does no harm and is obviously essential for some.

Others in the field of mathematics education have been and are now working to improve student learning in mathematics through that same lens. Susan Gay and Steven White (2002), at the University of Kansas, write of their efforts to help algebra students understand and communicate their mathematical ideas. The research they've surveyed and their work with local teachers convinces them that "vocabulary-building strategies can help young adolescents better understand the mathematical concepts they are being asked to learn" (33).

Mahesh Sharma (2002), director of the Center for Teaching/Learning Mathematics in Framingham, Massachusetts, has worked for years on the problems of students diagnosed with *dyscalculia*, the inability to conceptualize numbers, number relationships, and outcomes of numerical operations. One of the related environmental factors he has identified is the inadequate development of mathematical language. This is important information for special-education teachers working with students who might have this type of learning disability, which is proving to be more prevalent than dyslexia.

Lelon Capps and Jamar Pickreign describe several interesting vocabulary-building strategies in *Language Connections in Mathematics: A Critical Part of Mathematics Instruction* (1993). They use word-analysis activities and incorporate contextual activities that highlight the specialized nature of mathematical terms. But they go much further than I have dared. They feel that the language of mathematics must become part of other areas of the curriculum as well. For those working in self-contained classrooms or those working in teams, this holds great promise. Having tried to implement such strategies in departmentalized situations over the years, I can only attest to frustration.

As you create and/or recreate your mathematics classroom, you need to proceed in a thoughtful, reflective manner. Use a topological map like Ritchhart's list of "cultural forces" or a similar tool to guide you. Be cognizant of what your students need. Look into their eyes, listen to their responses, and learn with them. Ask yourself these questions:

◆ What are your expectations for student learning and thinking with regard to mathematics?

- What routines and structures will you employ to guide the class?
- How will you use the language of mathematics and encourage conversation and discussion?
- What different kinds of learning opportunities will you create to ensure mathematical learning for all your students?
- How will you model using and learning mathematics?
- What are the attitudes you want to convey to your students about learning mathematics?
- What relationships and interactions do you want to foster within your classroom between and among students and between you and your students?
- What are the important physical elements of the classroom and how will you organize them to maximize student opportunities to learn mathematics?

In building his case for the importance of these cultural forces Ritchhart writes about the power of language:

> Language wraps itself around, in, through, and between everything that we teachers and learners do in the classroom. Because it is omnipresent, we can easily take the role of language for granted, considering it only as a tool for delivering our content. Yet in many ways language acts as both the medium and the message in the cultivation of intellectual character. (141–42)

In 1990 Rebecca Corwin, Senior Associate at TERC (Technical Education Resource Centers), recommended a process approach to mathematics similar to a process approach for writing.

> Consider mathematics as malleable! Writers shape words to communicate; so do mathematicians. We can and should be using a process approach to mathematics instruction so that students can explore the world of mathematical communication on their own terms. (19)

The vocabulary of mathematics is the foundation of its language. Indeed, the words of mathematics are the clay with which students sculpt their mathematical ideas and understanding (Gay and White 2002). Using diverse opportunities such as those represented throughout this book as windows, doors, and secret passageways, mathematics vocabulary and concepts are revealed.

Bibliography

ACQUARELLI, K. 1992. "Growing in Four Steps: Growth Sequences with a Calculator Taught by Michael White." *Math Solutions Newsletter* 13 (Spring/Summer): 8–9.

ALLEN, J. 1999. *Words, Words, Words*. York, ME: Stenhouse.

ANNO, M., AND M. ANNO. 1983. *Anno's Mysterious Multiplying Jar*. New York: Philomel.

ASSOCIATION OF TEACHERS OF MATHEMATICS IN MAINE (ATOMIM). 2000. *I Have, Who Has?* (Winter): 11.

ATWELL, N. 1998. *In the Middle: New Understandings About Writing, Reading, and Learning*. Portsmouth, NH: Heinemann.

BAKER, S.K., D.C. SIMONS, AND E.J. KAMEENUI. 1995. *Vocabulary Acquisition: Synthesis of the Research*. Technical Report No. 13. University of Oregon: National Center to Improve the Tools for Educators.

BIGGERSTAFF, M., B. HALLORAN, AND C. SERRANO. 1994. "Use Color to Assess Mathematics Problem Solving." *Arithmetic Teacher* 41 (6): 307–8.

BLACHOWICZ, C., AND P. FISHER. 1996. *Teaching Vocabulary in All Classrooms*. Upper Saddle River, NJ: Prentice-Hall.

BRANDT, R. 1993. "On Teaching for Understanding: A Conversation with Howard Gardner." *Educational Leadership* 50 (7): 4–7.

BURNS, M. 1987. *A Collection of Lessons from Grades 3 Through 6*. Sausalito, CA: Math Solutions Publications.

———. 1991. *Writing in the Math Class*. Sausalito, CA: Math Solutions Publications.

———. 1995. *Writing in the Math Class*. Sausalito, CA: Math Solutions Publications.

———. 1996. *50 Problem-Solving Lessons, Grades 1–6*. Sausalito, CA: Math Solutions Publications.

BURNS, M., AND C. MCLAUGHLIN. 1990. *A Collection of Lessons from Grades 6 through 8*. Sausalito, CA: Math Solutions Publications.

BURNS, M., AND B. TANK. 1988. *A Collection of Lessons from Grades 1 through 3*. Sausalito, CA: Math Solutions Publications.

CALIFORNIA ASSESSMENT PROGRAM. 1989. *A Question of Thinking: A First Look at Students' Performance on Open-ended Questions in Mathematics.* Sacramento, CA: California Department of Education.

CAPPS, L.R., AND J. PICKREIGN. 1993. "Language Connections in Mathematics: A Critical Part of Mathematics Instruction." *Arithmetic Teacher* 41 (1): 8–12.

CAPPS, L.R., AND M.S. GAGE. 1987. "Mathematics Spoken Here: A Case for Language and Vocabulary Instruction in Mathematics" In *Current Issues in Mathematics*. Boston: Houghton Mifflin.

CART, M. 2001. "Poetry Changes the World" *Carte Blanche. Booklist* 15 March, 1390. Published by American Library Association.

CHANDLER, K.L., ed. 2001. *2001–2002 MATHCOUNTS School Handbook*. Alexandria, VA: MATHCOUNTS Foundation.

———, ed. 2002. *2002–2003 MATHCOUNTS School Handbook*. Alexandria, VA: MATHCOUNTS Foundation.

COATES, G.D., AND V. THOMPSON. 2003. *FAMILY MATH II: Achieving Success in Mathematics*. Berkeley, CA: The Regents of the University of California.

CORWIN, R.B. 1990. "A Process Approach to Mathematics: Mathematics as Communication." *HANDS ON!* 13 (1): 1, 19.

COUNTRYMAN, J. 1992. *Writing to Learn Mathematics*. Portsmouth, NH: Heinemann.

DOWN, A.G. 1997. "Getting to No. 1: Some Reflections on the Third International Mathematics and Science Study." *Education Week*. March 26, 56.

DOWNIE, D., T. SLESNICK, AND J.K. STENMARK. 1981. *Math for Girls and Other Problem Solvers.* Berkeley, CA: EQUALS, Lawrence Hall of Science.

DYKSTRA, J., AND A.F. FEGE. 1997. "Not Without Parents." *Education Week.* March 19, 60, 44.

EDUCATION DEVELOPMENT CENTER, INC. 1994. *The Language of Numbers. Seeing and Thinking Mathematically in the Middle Grades* series. Portsmouth, NH: Heinemann.

ENZENSBERGER, H.M. 1998. *The Number Devil: A Mathematical Adventure.* New York: Henry Holt & Company.

ENYART, A.M., AND L.R. VAN ZOEST. 1998. "Mathematics the Write Way." In *Mathematics in the Middle,* edited by Larry Leutzinger. Reston, VA: NCTM.

ERICKSON, T. 1989. *Get It Together: Math Problems for Groups, Grades 4–12.* Berkeley, CA: EQUALS, Lawrence Hall of Science.

FENDEL, D., D. RESEK, L. ALPER, AND S. FRASER. 1998. *It's All Write. Interactive Mathematics Program* series. Emeryville, CA: Key Curriculum Press.

GARDNER, H. 1983. *Frames of Mind: The Theory of Multiple Intelligences.* New York: Basic Books.

GAY, A.S., AND S.H. WHITE. 2002. "Teaching Vocabulary to Communicate Mathematically." *Middle School Journal* 34 (2): 33–38.

HEDDENS, J.W., AND W.R. SPEER. 2000. *Today's Mathematics, Part 1 & 2.* Hoboken, NJ: Jossey-Bass.

HENDERSON, A., AND N. BERLA. 1994. *A New Generation of Evidence: The Family Is Critical to Student Achievement.* Washington, DC: National Committee for Citizens in Education.

HOUSE, P.A. 1996. "Try a Little of the Write Stuff." In *Communication in Mathematics, K–12 and Beyond,* edited by Portia C. Elliott and Margaret J. Kenney. Reston, VA: NCTM.

ISDELL, W.D. 1993. *A Gebra Named Al.* Minneapolis, MN: Free Spirit Publishing.

JENSEN, E. 1998. *Teaching with the Brain in Mind.* Alexandria, VA: Association for Supervision and Curriculum Development.

JOHNSON, H.C. 1944. "The Effect of Instruction in Mathematical Vocabulary

Upon Problem Solving in Arithmetic." *Journal of Educational Research* 38: 97–110.

KAUFMAN, M.T. 1998. "A Billion, A Trillion, Whatever." *New York Times*, 18 October, Section 4, p. 2.

LAPPAN, G., J.T. FEY, W.M. FITZGERALD, S. FRIEL, AND E.D. PHILLIPS. 2002a. *Accentuate the Negative. Connected Mathematics* series. Glenview, IL: Prentice Hall.

———. 2002b. *Bits and Pieces II. Connected Mathematics* series. Glenview, IL: Prentice Hall.

———. 2002c. *Covering and Surrounding. Connected Mathematics* series. Glenview, IL: Prentice Hall.

———. 2002d. *Filling and Wrapping. Connected Mathematics* series. Glenview, IL: Prentice Hall.

———. 2002e. *Variables and Patterns. Connected Mathematics* series. Glenview, IL: Prentice Hall.

LYDA, W.J., AND T.M. DUNCAN. 1967. "Quantitative Vocabulary and Problem Solving." *Arithmetic Teacher* 14: 289–91.

MASSACHUSETTS DEPARTMENT OF EDUCATION. 2000. *MCAS Release of Spring 2000 Test Items*. Open response item 8, Grade 8 mathematics. Malden, MA: The Commonwealth of MA Department of Education.

THE MATHEMATICAL ASSOCIATION (U.K.). 1987. *Math Talk*. Portsmouth, NH: Heinemann.

NATIONAL COUNCIL OF SUPERVISORS OF MATHEMATICS (NCSM). 1997. *Supporting Improvement in Mathematics Education: A Public Relations Source Book*. Page II-H-16 from a presentation given by Dr. William Speer at ECTM, Ramstein, Germany. October, 1994. Golden, CO: NCSM.

NATIONAL COUNCIL OF TEACHERS OF MATHEMATICS (NCTM). 1989. *Curriculum and Evaluation Standards for School Mathematics*. Reston, VA: NCTM.

———. 2000. *Principles and Standards for School Mathematics*. Reston, VA: NCTM.

———. 1991. *Professional Standards for Teaching Mathematics*. Reston, VA: NCTM.

NURNBERG, M. 1998. *I Always Look Up the Word "E-gre-gious."* New York: Barnes and Noble.

OLIVER, M. 1995. *Blue Pastures.* New York: Harcourt Brace & Company.

PAPPAS, T. 1991. *Math Talk: Mathematical Ideas in Poems for Two Voices.* San Carlos, CA: Wide World Publishing/Terra.

RITCHHART, R. 2002. *Intellectual Character: What It Is, Why It Matters, and How to Get It.* San Francisco, CA: Jossey-Bass.

ROSEBERY, A.S., AND B. WARREN. 2001. "Children's Ways with Words." *HANDS ON!* 24 (1): 14, 16–17.

RUBENSTEIN, R.N. 1996. "Strategies to Support the Learning of the Language of Mathematics." In *Communication in Mathematics, K–12 and Beyond,* edited by Portia C. Elliott and Margaret J. Kenney. Reston, VA: NCTM.

SCHWARTZMAN, S. 1994. *The Words of Mathematics: An Etymological Dictionary of Mathematical Terms Used in English.* Washington, DC: The Mathematical Association of America.

SHANAHAN, J.M. 1999. *The Most Brilliant Thoughts of All Time (In Two Lines or Less).* New York: HarperCollins.

SHARMA, M., AND P. BRAZIL. 2002. "Dyscalculia." In *Berkshire Mathematics.* *www.dyscalculia.org/BerkshireMath.html.*

SIMPSON, J.B. 1988. *Simpson's Contemporary Quotations: The Most Notable Quotes Since 1950.* Boston: Houghton Mifflin.

STENMARK, J.K., AND THE EQUALS STAFF. 1989. *Assessment Alternatives in Mathematics.* Berkeley, CA: Lawrence Hall of Science.

STENMARK, J.K., ed. 1991. *Mathematics Assessment: Myths, Models, Good Questions, and Practical Suggestions.* Reston, VA: NCTM.

SULLIVAN, P., AND P. LILBURN. 2002. *Good Questions for Math Teaching: Why Ask Them and What to Ask, K–6.* Sausalito, CA: Math Solutions Publications.

SUTTON, S. 1998. "Formula for Success." *Newsday* 28 November, B.

THIER, M., AND B. DAVISS. 2002. *The New Science Literacy: Using Language Skills to Help Students Learn Science.* Portsmouth, NH: Heinemann.

USISKIN, Z. 1996. "Mathematics as a Language." In *Communication in Math-*

ematics, K–12 and Beyond, edited by Portia C. Elliott and Margaret J. Kenney. Reston, VA: NCTM.

WILLINGHAM, D.T. 2002. "Allocating Student Study Time: 'Massed' versus 'Distributed' Practice." *American Educator* 26 (2): 37–39.

WINGERT, P. 1996. "Education—The Sum of Mediocrity: In Math, Americans Finish Way Out of the Money." *Newsweek* 2 December, 96.

Index

Addition
  terminology, 35
Allen, Janet
  direct vocabulary instruction, 4
Area and perimeter
  demons, 78–81
Assessment(s)
  conceptual development, 5
  conversation rubric, 57
  group work, 59
  informal, 24
  reflection, 103
  state, 86
Assessment and evaluation
  activities category, 169, 173
Atwell, Nancie, 131–32, 157

Baker, S. K., 4
Behavioral norms
  group work, 51
Binary operations, 62–63, 64–69
Binder organization
  day one, 15–18
  guidelines, 16–18
Biweekly self-evaluation, 17
Blachowicz, Camille, 5, 21–22, 133–34, 151, 168, 169
Brain research, 11, 49
Brainstorm
  problem solving, 58
  rubric development, 56–57, 104–5
  vocabulary, 143, 179
Burns, Marilyn, 11, 40, 89

Capps, Lelon, 4
Categories for strategies, 169
  assessment and evaluation, 173
  classroom culture, 171–72
  classroom management, 170–71
  classroom rituals, 172

specific vocabulary activities, 173–74
Choice
  genre, 143
  special assignment terms, 143
  vocabulary words, 27
Clarifying terms
  poetry, 154
Classroom
  audit, 178
  climate, 15–21
  conversation rubric, 56–58
  culture, 169, 171–72, 177–78
  environment, 5
  management, 169, 170–71
  rituals, 2, 169, 172
Collaboration
  minilessons, 61–63
  problem solving, 38
  writing reflections, 104
Communicating mathematically, 1, 4, 8, 11, 109–13
Commutative property, 29, 64–65, 67, 144, 147
Concept maps, 71, 74–78
Conceptual development, 95, 103, 121–22, 135
Conceptual understanding,
  analogies and metaphors, 154
  built with vocabulary, 5, 60–61, 85, 88, 146, 168
  concept maps, 71, 74–78
  evidence of, 133–136, 138–41
  linear relationships, 136, 138
  poetry, 153, 162
  reflections, 103
Conjectures, 3, 42
Connected Mathematics
  Accentuate the Negative, 95, 109–11
  Bits and Pieces II, 42–44, 53–54
  Covering and Surrounding, 117, 120

explanation prompts, 86
  Filling and Wrapping, 111–13
  investigations, 102–3
  Moving Straight Ahead, 138
  Variables and Patterns, 103–7
Connecting: Math and Writing, 176–77
Context, vocabulary study, 4, 25
Cooperative learning problems, 51–52
Corresponding, 41
Countryman, Joan, 89, 133, 153
Creativity, 143, 153
Cultural forces/elements, 177–78, 183
Cumulative record, 135

Daily
  journal entries, 132
  reflections, 16, 53, 117, 122–24
Day
  one, 15–18
  two, 18–19
  three, 19–20
Definitions
  broad meanings, 162
  role of, 23
  special vocabulary assignment, 144
  student, 27, 69
  use of, 133, 135
Demons, 61, 78–81
Dictionary(ies)
  definitions, 25, 133–35
  resources, 19
  use of, 27, 45, 69, 169
Digits
  Maximum/minimum Products, 89–91
Discourse
  classroom, 34
  professional standards, 36
  using questions, 40–42, 45
Distributed practice, 61, 70
Distributive property, 23, 24, 133, 134

Doors, 22, 61, 142–49
Duncan, T. M., 4
Dyscalculia, 183

Ebbinghaus, Hermann, 61
Elegant
    definition, 24, 69
    poetry, 144, 146, 147–48, 156, 165, 166
    rubric descriptor, 92–93, 105, 111
Entries
    evaluation, 29
    weekly vocabulary, 27–29
Erickson, Tim, 51–52
Etymology
    linear, 78
    mathematics, 21
    poetry, 154
Evaluating mathematical statements,
    113–15
Evaluation, 123, 125–26
Everyday Mathematics, 40
Evidence
    arguments, 57–58, 86, 91, 132–41
    long range benefits, 178–82
    of thinking, 166
    of understanding, 115
    value of vocabulary, 175–76
Examples, 121, 136, 139–41
Expectations
    class conversations, 56–59
    a cultural force, 177
    participation, 178
    performance, 58–59
    small group work, 51–53
    for students, 15–16
    student self-evaluation, 136
Exponents, 37–39
Exponential
    form, 38
    growth, 49

Factor, 16, 38–39
Factor versus multiple, 78, 80–81
Factorials, 49
FAMILY MATH, 13, 14
Fisher, Peter, 5, 21–22, 133–34, 151, 168, 169
Format
    Haiku, 160
    mathematics write-up, 91
    tritina, 160
Formative evaluation, 132–35

Gage, Martha, 4
Gardner, Howard, 166–67
Generalizing, 91
Geometry activity
    "Build a Structure," 49–50
Goals
    assessment cycle, 173
    setting, 136

Good Questions for Math Teaching, 40
Group summary, 42–45
Group work, 37, 39–40, 51–53
Guidelines
    journal and binder, 18–19, 116–17, 121–23
    vocabulary program, 21–23, 169

Haiku
    format, 160
    poetry workshop, 157–60, 161, 164, 165
Homework
    assignments, 127–29, 162–63
    binder section, 16–17
    log, 18, 90, 126–28, 133
    long term, 91
    processing, 130
    role in curriculum, 5
    self-evaluation, 133–34
House, Peggy, 89, 143
Hypotenuse, 2, 161

"I Have, Who Has?", 55, 63, 69–70, 72–73, 180
Imagery, 154
Immersion, 12, 21–23, 35, 60, 170
Independent
    learners, 15
    thinking, 100
Integer operations, 113–15
Integers, 45, 63, 95–98, 100, 109–11, 157–59
Inventory
    trimester self-evaluation, 135–41
Inverse relationships, 62–63, 64–69
Investigation, 102–7
Investigations
    standards-based curriculum, 40
Irrational numbers, 159, 164–65

Jensen, Eric, 11
Johnson, Harry C., 4
Journal
    folder, 125
    student binder, 16, 17, 90

Kameenui, E. J., 4–5
Knowing a word, 23, 168

Language, 12, 60–61, 177
Learning community, 177
Linear, 78–79
Linguistic disadvantage, 11–12
Listening, 55–56, 179
Literature, 46–49
Lyda, W. J., 4

MATHCOUNTS
    binder section, 17, 18
    problems, 2, 37

as resource, 40, 81
    student recollections, 180
Math in Context
    standards-based curriculum, 40
Math poem development, 159, 160, 162
MathScape
    standards-based curriculum, 40
Math survey, 19–21
Mathematics
    curriculum, 5
    definition, 21
Mathematically powerful, 3–4
MATHThematics
    standards-based curriculum, 40
Mathematics vocabulary, 15–16, 20–23
Meaningful use
    biweekly self-evaluations, 132–35
    importance, 22, 36
    journals, 122
    math language, 71, 75, 78
    math poetry, 162
    math reflections, 111
    opportunities, 22, 23
    problem solving, 39–40
    special vocabulary assignments, 142–49
    writing, 85–86, 100–1
Metacognition, 42, 131, 180
Metaphors
    and analogies, 154
    creating, 162
    poetry, 144, 157, 164
Million model, 46
Minilesson(s)
    from assignments, 148
    based on reflections, 102
    four operations, 62–63, 64–69
    from journal evaluations, 125, 127
    mathematical statements, 113–15
    note taking, 117–22
    volume and surface area, 121–22
Multiple intelligences, 166–67
Multiplicative inverse, 63, 65

National Council of Teachers of
    Mathematics
    Curriculum and Evaluation Standards,
        12, 60
    Principles and Standards for School
        Mathematics, 23, 24, 42, 85
    Professional Standards for Teaching
        Mathematics, 36
Necessary and sufficient, 24, 69, 92
New York Times
    "A Billion, A Trillion, Whatever," 46,
        47–48
Note taking
    journal, 16, 117–22
    listening skills, 56
    minilesson, 121
    skill development, 63

Number sense, 3, 46
Number system
  place value, 46
  understanding, 2

Oliver, Mary, 156–57, 160
Opportunity(ies)
  cultural force, 177
  meaningful encounters, 147
Operations (four)
  concept maps, 71, 74–75
  minilessons, 62–63, 64–69
Organization
  binder, 15–18
  classroom, 19

Pairs, 49–50
Pappas, Theoni, 48, 180
Paraphrasing
  listening skills, 56
  student recollection, 179
Parents
  beliefs, 13
  homework log, 126–28
  involvement, 5, 16, 41
  letter to, 12–14
  portfolio conferences, 75
  trimester self-evaluation, 135–36
Participation
  biweekly self-evaluations, 133
  paraphrasing, 56
  vocabulary day, 27, 179
Patterns
  describing, 95, 113, 115
  in literature, 49
  long range impact, 175
  and relationships, 3, 44–45
Peer
  coaching, 50, 69
  review, 69, 94–95, 107–9
Personal vocabulary, 16, 26–34
Place value, 2, 35, 46, 46–48, 91
Poetry, 46–48, 143, 144, 147–48
Portfolio
  conferences, 71, 75, 78, 135–36
  homework log sample, 128
  learning list, 122, 125
  preparation, 17, 63, 71, 74–75
  what helps students learn, 148–49
Power
  of language, 184
  mathematical, 3–4
  poetry and mathematics, 157
Prime
  factor, 38, 39
  factorization, 38–39
  number, 38, 39
Prioritizing, 56
Prisms, 5, 6–7, 111–12, 161
Problem solving write-ups, 18–19, 180

Problems
  An Exploration into Sums, 95–98, 100
  generating conversation, 37, 39–40
  Growing in Four Steps, 99–100
  Maximum and Minimum Products, 89–91
Processing
  biweekly self-evaluations, 133
  homework, 130
  special vocabulary assignment, 144–46
Prompts
  for evaluating statements, 113–15
  Mathematical Reflections, 103, 109–10, 111
  self-evaluation, 132–41

Questions, 40–45

Read–aloud
  A Gebra Named Al, 143–44
Reading response, 129–30
Record keeping
  biweekly self-evaluations, 132
  journal, 117–23
Reflection, 132
Regional units, 80
Relation, 36
Relationships
  between concepts, 168
  describing, 180
  student/teacher, 178
Research record, 4–5, 11, 13, 61
Resources
  classroom (locating), 18–19
  questions, 40
Responsibility
  student, 12, 15, 136
  teacher, 15
Ritchhart, Ron, 175, 177–78, 182, 183–84
Rituals
  brainstorming, 56–57, 58, 104–5, 143, 179
  daily math reflections, 122–24
  self-assessment, 132–41
  write-ups, 89–101
  writing, 85
Routines
  a cultural force, 177
  participation, 178
Rubenstein, Rheta N., 60, 154
Rubric
  classroom conversation, 56–58
  listening, 55
  mathematical reflections, 104–5, 107
  writing guide, 92–94
Safe environment, 15
Schwartzman, Steven, 9, 78
Secret passageways, 22–23
Self-assessment (teacher)
  classroom audit, 178, 183–84

Self-directed learning, 89
Self-evaluation
  biweekly, 132–35
  forms, 134, 137–41
  history and support, 131–32
  journal, 124, 126
Sharing,
  think-pair-share, 39, 40
  vocabulary assignments, 144–46
Silence, 36
Similarity
  concept maps, 75–78
  partner work, 50
  poetry, 154–56, 162, 163
Simons, D. C., 4–5
Slope, 5, 8, 138
Spacing effect
  cognitive research, 61
  spaced practice, 70
Specific vocabulary activities
  category of strategies, 169, 173–74
Spokesperson, 53
Square roots (in literature), 49
Standards-based curriculums, 40
Standards, 3, 12, 23–24, 36, 42, 60, 85
Stenmark, Jean Kerr, 131
Student questions, 45
Student responsibility
  distractions, 56
  homework log, 126–28
  learning, 132–35
Student as teacher, 154–63
Student work, 117–24
Subversive activities, 23, 41, 42
Surface area, 5, 6–7, 102–8, 111–12, 124
Summary(ies), 86, 104, 105, 117–24
Summary
  trimester self-evaluation, 135
Summative self-evaluation, 135–41

Terminology, 9
Thier, Marlene, 58–59
Think, pair, share, 36
Thinking
  use of language, 42
  writing and talking about, 12
Tritina
  format, 160
  poetry workshop, 157–66

Unit perspective, 136, 138
Usiskin, Zal, 12

Value (of poetry), 166
Vocabulary acquisition
  getting started, 12–21
  implications of research, 36
  planning for, 23–26
  support for, 5

Vocabulary acquisition (*continued*)
  self-assessment, 132–41
  thesis of book, 1
Vocabulary assignments
  poetry lesson, 162–63
  special, 142–49, 153, 154
  student recollections, 180
Vocabulary brainstorm, 17, 26
Vocabulary day, 27
Vocabulary development
  conversation, 37–49
  self-evaluation, 136–41
  success in mathematics, 4
  use of questions, 40–45
Vocabulary instruction, 4
Vocabulary lessons
  "doors", 61
Vocabulary lists
  cooperative learning problem, 51–53
  linear relationships, 100

special vocabulary assignment, 144
  typical academic year, 32
Vocabulary perspective
  trimester self-evaluation, 138–41
Vocabulary practice
  journals, 121
  research on, 61
Vocabulary record, 26–34
Vocabulary research, 169
Vocabulary scavenger hunt, 13
Vocabulary section (binder), 17
Vocabulary work, 148
Volume, 5, 6–7, 108, 111–12

Whole class, 53–55
Whole number operations, 61–63, 64–69
Window(s)
  into depth of thinking, 95
  different ways to learn, 167
  doors, and secret passageways, 185

level of vocabulary work, 22–23
  words as, 1
Word knowledge, 23
Word list
  typical academic year, 32
Word wall
  folder, 17
  index, 26, 27–30
  self-evaluation, 136
  student recollection, 179
Workshop
  poetry and mathematics, 154–66
Writing in mathematics
  benefits, 88–89
  conference, 161
  math journals, 16
  math poem, 160–62
  opportunities and resources, 89
  problem solving, 18
  tool for learning, 85

Continued from page ii.